UNDERSTANDING
THE **PURPOSE** AND **POWER** OF

WOMEN

DR. MYLES MUNROE

UNDERSTANDING

THE **PURPOSE** AND **POWER** OF

WOMEN

GOD'S DESIGN FOR FEMALE IDENTITY

EXPANDED EDITION WITH STUDY GUIDE

WHITAKER
HOUSE

UNDERSTANDING THE PURPOSE AND POWER OF WOMEN:
God's Design for Female Identity
(Expanded Edition with Study Guide)

Munroe Global
P.O. Box N9583
Nassau, Bahamas
www.munroeglobal.com
office@munroeglobal.com

ISBN: 978-1-64123-014-8
eBook ISBN: 978-1-60374-149-1
Printed in the United States of America
© 2001, 2018 by Munroe Group of Companies Ltd.

Whitaker House
1030 Hunt Valley Circle
New Kensington, PA 15068
www.whitakerhouse.com

The Library of Congress has cataloged the original trade paper edition as follows:

Munroe, Myles.
Understanding the purpose and power of woman / by Myles Munroe.
p.   cm.
ISBN 0-88368-671-6 (pbk. : alk. paper)
1. Women—Religious aspects—Christianity.   I. Title.
BT704 .M86 2001
261.8'344—dc21
2001003223

1 2 3 4 5 6 7 8 9 10 ᴜᴊ 24 23 22 21 20 19 18

DEDICATION

To my friend, partner, and darling wife, Ruth, a woman who has become the embodiment of the qualities and principles in this work. Her love, respect, support, and confidence in me over the many years of marriage have helped me to understand the gift and essence of womanhood.

To my beloved daughter Charisa, to whom I have dedicated my life to being a mortal father and mentor with the hope that she will become the quality of woman like her mother and someday be a wife of noble worth to a God-fearing man.

To my beloved sisters, Sheila, Verdel, Suzan, Christine, Deborah, Venessa, and Adine, with whom I grew up and from whom I have learned the essence of the female factor.

And to the women of the developing third-world nations who, for many years, have been the victims of social, cultural, economic, and spiritual oppression. May you discover and experience the joy of dignity, equality, and fulfillment that were created in you.

ACKNOWLEDGMENTS

Every accomplishment in life is a result of the contribution of many individuals who both directly and indirectly share their gifts, talents, and wisdom with us all. This project is no exception. I am indebted to my beloved wife, Ruth, and my late mother, Louise Munroe, who exemplify the ideals of motherhood and nobility of womanhood, and to my precious children, Charisa and Chairo. I also want to thank my editor at Whitaker House, Lois Smith Puglisi, who, in the relentless pursuit of truth and clarity, persevered through the demands of my hectic travel schedule and project deadlines to get this book to you. I appreciate all of the women at Bahamas Faith International Fellowship who have applied these principles throughout the years through my teaching programs. Most of all, I am grateful to the Creator of both male and female who has blessed us with all of our gifts.

CONTENTS

INTRODUCTION

It is extremely difficult to be a woman in the twenty-first century. Women around the world are facing the dilemma of identity. Many women are struggling to discover who they are and where they stand today—in the family, the community, and the world. At the same time that women's personal expectations and roles are changing in some nations, many men around the world still have their own opinions about the place of women and want to impose certain standards of behavior on them. Other men are uncertain about the woman's role and function, and therefore they offer little support to women who are struggling with questions of identity. Additionally, many societies are still very much in a place of transition regarding the status of women. Because of this shift in position and roles, many women are finding themselves in either an uneasy cooperation or an uncomfortable conflict with men.

The question of a woman's status and the issue of equal rights for women are relevant to every culture and society on the globe. The world's confusion over the place and worth of women manifests itself in a variety of ways. In industrial nations, changing roles of women in the family and society not only have brought new vocational opportunities for women but also unforeseen personal and social issues. Even though women are working the same jobs as men, on average they earn less than men and have less opportunity for advancement. Though many women are building careers, they are also still doing the majority of the child-rearing and household chores. The pace of such a life is leaving them exhausted and disillusioned. On a personal level, confusion over male/female roles and expectations has led to misunderstandings, conflicts, and unstable relationships with the opposite sex. Women today are struggling with the delicate balance of attending to the needs of both their families and their careers, job competition with men, emotional turmoil and lost income due to divorce, single parenthood, and conflicts stemming from cultural changes in the way women and men interrelate. Some women are confused about what a woman should be and how she should conduct herself because they're not sure what a woman is supposed to be responsible for anymore.

> **WE ARE NOT ADDRESSING THE UNDERLYING CAUSE OF THE PROBLEMS OF WOMEN WORLDWIDE.**

What is compounding these issues is that cultures around the world have their own ideas about a woman's identity and role, and these ideas are varied and contradictory. In many Western countries, a woman is accepted as a competitor in the work world at the same time she is often expected to fulfill the traditional roles of wife and mother. In many developing countries, cultural views of a woman's role continue to devalue her worth and dignity. Sometimes, she's considered the equivalent of a domestic servant or slave. A woman living under such a view is extremely vulnerable to emotional or physical abuse, poverty, disease, and even death. A striking example of this is the plight of women in Afghanistan who are being denied health care, education, employment, and personal freedoms. Another example is the situation of women in third-world nations who are at high risk of contracting HIV/AIDS. The June 2000 United Nations AIDS Report on the Global Epidemic reported that the percentage of women being infected with HIV is rising. Fifty-two percent (1.3 million) of all AIDS deaths in the year 2000 were women. The reason? Many young girls and women are being sexually exploited and are falling victim to the disease through contact with infected men.

The breadth and depth of the issues that women face worldwide is overwhelming. Yet current books and other literature about male-female relationships and women's rights are not addressing the underlying cause that is fueling the crises women are dealing with today. My concern is that the longer this cause is overlooked, the longer the plight of women will continue.

I travel throughout the world, and I see the numerous problems of women firsthand. Women are facing a myriad of issues and dilemmas, whether they live in Africa, Europe, the Caribbean, South America,

Australia, Antarctica, Asia, or North America. There will always be certain factors, such as natural disasters and war, that exasperate problems for women and men alike; however, the *root cause* of the special problems women face, the issue that is largely contributing to their distress in the world, is essentially being ignored. The woman in North America who is juggling a career and family, the woman in Afghanistan who is being denied basic human rights, and the young girl in Kenya who has just contracted the AIDS virus are each facing aspects of a common dilemma. Their problems are different manifestations of an underlying issue. Uncovering and addressing this underlying issue is a central theme of this book. What, then, is the root cause of the problem?

Before I answer this question, I want to say that it is not as if efforts and progress have not been made in respecting and valuing women. For example, from its inception, the United Nations has been concerned with women's issues. The United Nations charter affirms its "faith in fundamental human rights, in the dignity and worth of the human person, in the equal rights of men and women." In the years since the founding of the United Nations, international laws and treaties regarding women's rights have been adopted. Yet if you read the language of these succeeding proclamations, you will notice a recurring theme. After acknowledging that some progress has been made, the resolutions admit that discrimination against women still exists—even among member nations who have pledged to uphold the resolutions! Those who are committed to making life better for women have had to admit that progress is slow and that change is hard to measure—and even harder to enforce.

The UN Convention on the Elimination of All Forms of Discrimination against Women, often called the "international bill of rights for women," suggests the cause of the problem. It "targets culture and tradition as influential forces shaping gender roles and family relations." Over the centuries and millennia, societies all over the world have developed ideas about what it means to be a woman or a man, and most of what has been promoted through culture and tradition has devalued women in some way. We may well ask the question, What has caused diverse cultures and traditions around the world to misunderstand and devalue women? Why is this attitude seemingly ingrained in people's hearts the world over?

> IF YOU DON'T KNOW HOW SOMETHING IS MEANT TO FUNCTION, YOU WILL MISUSE OR ABUSE IT.

The basic problem can be summarized in this way: There are fundamental truths about the inherent makeup of women and men that have been lost to the cultures and traditions of the world as well as the hearts and minds of individual men and women. They have been replaced with distorted views of women and of male-female relationships, and these distortions have been promoted through culture and tradition. Because of these lost truths, women and men alike do not understand a woman's nature, potential, role, and unique contribution to the world. The result is that women are misunderstood, held back from fulfilling their potential, and abused. The hurt, loss, trauma, and physical peril this has placed on women is tragic. There has been a terrible waste of life and potential over hundreds and thousands of years; this waste has been catastrophic not only for women, but also for men and human society as a whole.

Women and men alike must come to know the woman's true nature and purpose if we are to address the plight that has affected women throughout history and still affects them in the twenty-first century. Women, as well as men, must gain new perspectives of themselves, since women have largely developed their self-concepts from cultural traditions shaped by men who did not understand females.

One of the main points I want to emphasize in this book is that, if you don't know how something is meant to function, you will misuse or abuse it. This is easy enough for us to understand if we're talking about bouncing checks because we've failed to balance our checkbooks properly or allowing our cars to slowly deteriorate by neglecting to change the oil regularly. Yet a similar principle applies to our failure to understand the inherent nature of women (and men) and how we were created to function together as human beings. The woman has been misunderstood, misinterpreted, and manipulated for thousands of years. As a result, she has been and is being abused in societies throughout the world.

This is why so many past efforts on behalf of women have fallen short of success. This is why a country like Afghanistan can appear to be making progress in valuing women and then reverse itself. Merely insisting that women be treated right apparently will not change the false views of males and females that are ingrained in many men and women. People lack a basic understanding of the woman's nature, and wherever this lack of understanding exists, there will always be the misuse and abuse of the woman. Therefore, we not only need to affirm the worth of women, but we also need to lay new groundwork for understanding who a woman is and how she should be viewed and treated. Repeated resolutions from the United Nations or the efforts of concerned groups—notwithstanding their good intent—cannot ultimately change the hearts of men.

We must look beyond the cultures of the world and rediscover intrinsic truths about the nature of women and men. We must transcend tradition and recapture principles that can free women to be fulfilled and valued, regardless of their nationality or geographic location. We need to understand the inherent nature of a woman and the implications of that nature that will enable us to address her particular issues—whether she is trying to balance a career and family, struggling to regain basic human rights, or at risk of contracting HIV/AIDS.

If we look at the issue of women's rights from this perspective, it will give us the proper focus for solving the problems women face. Much of the discussion of women's rights centers on what a woman is capable of doing and what she should be allowed to do. I would like to suggest, however, that these questions, while important, are actually secondary questions. The fundamental question, from which all other questions can be addressed, is not so much what a woman does as *who she is*, and the implications of who she is. When we come to know who a woman is, then the roles that she takes on in life—whether she is a homemaker, a businesswoman, or a prime minister—will be seen in an entirely new light, and the conflicts between women and men over the status of women can begin to be resolved.

A final note of caution: The temptation for women who are being devalued by men in a specific instance or through societal discrimination is to want to dismiss men altogether or treat them in an adversarial way. Yet to do this would be to disregard the inherent makeup of women and men and how they are meant to function *together*. The end result of such an approach would be damaging to a woman's potential and advancement, and real progress would not be accomplished.

Noeleen Heyzer, executive director of the United Nations Development Fund for Women, said in a recent International Women's Day message, "What we want for the twenty-first century is a rekindling of hope, the capacity for women around the world to bring their dreams of equality of access, opportunity and rights, freedom from discrimination, related intolerance and peace to reality, a better world for all."

This book is indeed about a rekindling of hope for women in the twenty-first century. The truths contained within can create a better world for women and men—the world it was created to be.

—*Myles Munroe*

ONE

A WOMAN'S PLACE

And so is the world put back by the death of every one who has to
sacrifice the development of his or her peculiar gifts (which were
meant, not for selfish gratification, but for the improvement of
that world) to conventionality.
—Florence Nightingale

In the mid-1960s, James Brown came out with a song that exposed the
spirit of the age, entitled, "It's a Man's World." The song sold a million
copies. (I wonder who bought it?) James Brown was singing about an attitude that pervades the nations and cultures of the world. That attitude is,
in effect, "Even though women are here, this world was made for men. It's
designed for males. Women are just filling in where needed. You women
stay in your place; this is a man's world."

Does the world belong to men? If so, what place do women hold in it?

A CONTROVERSIAL ISSUE

One of the most controversial issues of our modern times—a topic
that has been debated with much discussion and dissension—is the role,
position, and rights of the woman. Historically, in nearly every nation and
culture, women have been regarded as inferior to men, holding a secondary
place in the world. The following are traditional perceptions of women that
still persist today. Women are considered…

+ inferior to men, second-class citizens.

+ objects   for   sensual   gratification alone.

+ weak; incapable of real strength.

+ lacking in intelligence and therefore having nothing to contribute to
  society.

+ the personal property of men, the equivalent of cattle.

+ personal servants, whose only purpose is to meet the needs of their masters.

+ domestic slaves, to be used as desired.

+ objects to be passed around until finished with, and then discarded.

+ subhuman.

+ deserving of abuse.

Depending on where you live in the world, your past experiences, and whether you are a woman or a man, the items on this list might shock you, offend you, be discounted by you, or serve as a painful reminder of what you are currently enduring.

If you live in an industrial nation that has seen significant improvements in the status of women and the opportunities open to her, you may not think these negative perceptions of women are relevant to your relationships or the interactions between males and females in your society. Yet the underlying assumptions behind them persist in every nation because they are not so much influenced by legislative and societal changes as they are by ingrained attitudes in the hearts and minds of men and women. Women are misunderstood and degraded around the world, and it is causing them emotional, physical, and spiritual distress.

A UNIVERSAL PROBLEM

For thousands of years, in nearly every culture and tradition in the world, women have been devalued and therefore mistreated in some way. What accounts for this outlook? Why is this problem so universal? The fact that the devaluing of women is so widespread across the globe points to a cause that goes much deeper than mere culture or tradition.

YOU CAN'T EASILY CHANGE A MAN'S MIND-SET.

One of the reasons the plight of the woman has been such a difficult issue to remedy is that it's not easy to change a man's mind about a woman's place in the world. The idea that this is a man's world is very deeply entrenched. Even though legislation might be passed or public policy might change, you can't easily change a man's mind-set. This internalized devaluing of women is the reason why women generally continue to be discounted and exploited in almost every society in the world, regardless of certain social and political advances. In industrial nations as well as developing nations, the plight of the female is still very real. It is tragic to have to admit this is true in our modern society.

In the neighborhood where I grew up, it was common for me to hear men saying, "Woman, do you know who I am? I'm the one who wears the pants around here!" That statement was supposed to imply who was in charge. These days, both men and women wear pants, so who is that statement talking about now? This spirit of male dominance, this attitude of, "Stay in your place. You have no say in this; you have no contribution to make. You have no sense, anyway," has pervaded our societies for thousands of years, and it is a spirit that still has a hold on many nations.

This prevailing attitude is the reason why the social and political advances of women—which on the surface seem to be victories—can become burdens to women because they are in reality only one-sided victories. For example, women can declare that they are equal with men, and society can try to enforce this equality, but the attitudes of men (and also other women) may not necessarily be in agreement with this change in status. This can cause perplexity, stress, and conflict. Thus, much confusion about the role of the woman still exists today.

WOMEN'S MOVEMENTS

Only in the relatively recent past, mainly in industrial nations, have people risen up and argued that the devaluing of women is not right. This protest has been manifested in various women's movements, such as the women's suffrage movement in the nineteenth and early twentieth centuries. Sometimes we forget that it is only recently that women were given the right to vote in many countries. We're not talking about two centuries ago; we're talking about eighty years ago even in America. Only recently have certain nations considered women viable and significant contributors to the mainstream of society.

Some of this change came about through expediency. Two world wars and the Great Depression altered people's perception of the role of women and their capabilities. While the men were off fighting wars or looking for work in other cities or states, women were needed to take on roles and jobs that men had traditionally performed. After the Second World War, men returned to their jobs, and many women were expected to return to their former roles, but the taboo against women working and contributing in areas such as business and government had been broken. Even though traditional views of women predominated, the culture had undergone a perceptible change.

In the last forty years or so, in America and in parts of Europe—in countries such as England, Sweden, and Norway—a spirit has risen up among women, a spirit counter to the prevailing attitude, which says, "We are equal to men. There is no difference between us." In America this spirit has been encapsulated in the phrase "equal rights." The equal rights movement came to the foreground in the 1960s and originally had certain goals in common with the civil rights movement. The spirit of the James Brown song, that we live in a man's world, gave this movement its impetus, and millions of women got on the bandwagon. "This is not a man's world," they said. "We are here, too." Thousands of women marched in front of the White House in Washington, D.C. They held big banners and placards and shouted in the streets. They held meetings in football stadiums and packed them to capacity. These women talked about passing the Equal Rights Amendment (ERA). They wanted to amend the Constitution of the United States to declare that "equality of rights under the law shall not be denied or abridged by the United States or by any state on account of sex." They were crying out to be given their rights to be equal to men. They wanted the same rights as men to participate in the world and to be to be involved in everything men are involved in.

WHOSE RIGHTS?

I was in college during this period of uprising and revolution, and I used to sit in class and listen to people debate the issue of women's rights. I would also sit and watch television in the lobby of the university, and I very clearly remember seeing these women standing up, shouting for their rights. Although I appreciated their overall concerns, something about their approach bothered me. What came to

IF YOU ASK SOMEBODY FOR SOMETHING, YOU ARE ADMITTING THEY HAVE IT.

my mind as I watched them was that if you ask somebody for something, you are admitting that they have it; if you have to demand something from someone, you are confessing that they own it. When you do that, you are devaluing yourself, because you are, in effect, relinquishing the possession of your rights to someone else.

This principle may be widely applied. For example, it pertains to race relations as well as to male-female relationships. If the white man asks the black man for something, then the white man is saying to the black man, "You have what I need." If the black man asks the white man for something, he's saying to the white man, "You possess what is mine." If the female asks the male for something, she's admitting that he has it. If the male asks the female for something, he's acknowledging that she controls it. When you go to another person or group of people in order to get something that you claim you need, you are admitting that that person or group has ownership of it.

Therefore, if I say to the government, "Give me my rights," I am admitting to the government, "You have jurisdiction over my rights." Laws delineating our rights can be good, but we must remember that laws can't grant us our rights; they can merely acknowledge the rights that we already have. I decided years ago, as a teenager, that nobody has the liberty to control my rights because my rights are God-given and inherent. Some people are amazed at my outlook. A black preacher came up to me one time and said, "Man, you're a different kind of black man." I said, "No, I am in control of whose opinions are important." There is a significant difference between *demanding* one's rights from someone and *displaying* the rights one already possesses. This is a critical principle to keep in mind as we explore the underlying reason for the devaluing of women. If we understand that the woman's position and rights in the world are inherent, it is going to change our approach to solving her plight worldwide.

Joseph is a good example of a person who displayed his rights in the way in which he thought and lived. His story is told in the book of Genesis. Joseph was falsely accused and put in jail. Yet he said to himself, "I'm not a prisoner," and he was soon put in charge of the whole prison. (See Genesis 39.) It's all about attitude. The Romans had Jesus bound in chains, but Jesus told Pilate, in essence, "I'm not bound; you're the one who is bound."

Pilate said, "Don't You know who I am?" Jesus answered, "I know who you are. You're a fool. You're being totally manipulated by history and prophecy. You can't kill Me; I don't give you the right to have the power to kill Me. No man takes My life. I am a free Man." (See John 19:1–16.) There are people in jail right now who are spiritually free, and there are people who have never been near a jail who only seem to be free. Inwardly, they are bound.

So, when you demand something, you have to be careful, because you might be subconsciously implying something. You might be suggesting that you don't really have any rights of your own. I want to ask women, Do you really want to go to men and say, "I demand equality with you," implying that they have the power to *make* you equal? That is a dangerous thing to say. If you convince me that I have the power and the right to make you a whole person, then you are in trouble, because I could use it to play games with you, to manipulate you. I could use it to get what I want. I could give you some freedoms, as I pleased—just enough to keep you in check—and withhold the rest. I believe that many people in movements for equality are inadvertently confessing that they have given over their rights to someone else.

PREJUDICE PERSISTS

Even so, countries such as America and Sweden have recently elevated the status of women through legislative acts, achieving a certain amount of societal change. After a difficult struggle, the woman—who was once mainly thought of as a "baby-bearer," "property," "servant-slave-maid," and someone who did the work men considered beneath them—now participates to some degree in both civic and political affairs. Her contribution is beginning to be appreciated. Many women are involved in opportunities and activities that were formerly reserved for males, such as leadership, management, and sports.

> WOMEN HAVE NOT BEEN ALLOWED TO DEVELOP THEIR FULL POTENTIAL.

However, although we can say that there has been some improvement, in most societies, women are still suffering the prejudice of the male against the female, and this bias continues to degrade women. Men's hearts cannot be changed by legislation. People are still reacting and adjusting to the legislative and civic changes that have been made over the last several decades so that, even though the law says, "Women are now equal to men," this doesn't mean that men think so. As a result, women are still being confused, misused, and abused. They are being frustrated and manipulated. The persistent devaluing of women continues to hold back progress, and women are being treated in every way *except* in the way God originally intended.

This depreciation of women is preventing them from living in the fullness of what God created them to be. There have been some notable examples of women throughout history who have been able to accomplish great things, display exceptional work and talent, and contribute much to society. Yet the majority of women have not been allowed to develop their unique personalities and gifts fully so that they may enrich their own lives, their families, their churches, their communities, and the world.

The serious problem we are facing, therefore, is that, not even the government can really do what needs to be done to remedy the devaluation of women, despite legislation and some positive social changes.

CAN NEGATIVE IDEAS ABOUT WOMEN BE CHANGED?

Can the world's negative perceptions of the woman be transformed? What is the cause of the universal devaluing of women in societies across the centuries and around the globe? Why is it sometimes so difficult for men and women to understand one another and to work together harmoniously in this world? Culture and tradition, while apparently part of the problem, cannot take the full blame, because the problem spans ages and cultures and seems to point to a deep-seated discord or adversarial relationship between men and women.

What, then, is the cause of this age-old dilemma? It is that we have lost what it means to be human. We have lost what it means to be male and female. An understanding of the essential makeup of human beings has been discarded or forgotten and has been replaced with distorted views of humanity. Culture and tradition have then contributed to the problem by perpetuating these distortions.

Women as well as men need to understand the inherent nature of the woman, because most women have developed their identity from men, and they do not see themselves as God does. Women have essentially become the products of the societies and traditions into which they were born and bred. As a woman, you might not like who you are, yet your self-concept probably came from the environment in which you were raised.

EQUAL AND DIFFERENT

If the nations of the world had understood God's purposes for women and men, they would have realized that the spirit of equal rights that

GOD HAS ALREADY MADE MEN AND WOMEN EQUAL.

demands equality from men was never intended by God, because He has already made men and women equal. Men and women were created equal. Men and women are equal. That's not for a senate or a congress or a cabinet or a parliament to decide. God already made this decision in creation. Again, when you allow others to declare who you are, you are submitting your rights to them, and you must be prepared for the consequences. Don't ever give anybody the right to say what kind of human value you have. Don't let anybody else tell you how much of a person you are. When you understand that equality is inherent and discover how it is to be manifested in your life, then you can begin to live in the full realm of that equality, regardless of what others tell you about yourself.

There's another point we need to carefully consider, because it is at the forefront of the current misunderstandings between females and males. Many of those who advocate equal rights say that there is no difference at all between women and men. Yet while women and men were created equal, they were also created different. This is part of their unique design. This statement may confuse some and anger others, because somehow we have come to believe that *different* means *inferior*. It is true that many societies have promoted the false view that because women have a different physical and emotional makeup, they are somehow inferior to men. A few women have adopted the attitude that men are inferior because they are different from women. Both views fail to appreciate, value, and celebrate the complementary differences between men and women.

In many spheres of life, we don't consider differences to be weaknesses but rather mutual strengths. In music, who is more important to a full symphony orchestra, a violin player or an oboe player? Both work together in harmony. In sports, who is more important to a medley relay, the swimmer who swims the breaststroke or the swimmer who swims the backstroke? Both have to be strong swimmers in their particular specialty, for a medley race cannot be swum with only one type of swimmer. The answer to the historical devaluing of women does not lie in declaring that there are no differences between females and males, but in recognizing and affirming their complementary differences. The problem is that we don't understand and accept these differences so they can be used in harmony.

THE CAUSE OF CONFLICT

When we don't understand and appreciate our God-given differences, we will inevitably have conflict. If the female doesn't understand why she is the way she is, and the male doesn't understand why he is the way he is, then three kinds of conflicts will occur. Women won't be able to successfully get along with other women, men won't be able to successfully get along with other men, and women and men won't be able to successfully get along with each other.

This misunderstanding and discord between women and men may be illustrated by the way many people approach marriage today. Most people are unprepared for the marriage relationship. They approach it in the same way that they buy

> MANY PEOPLE APPROACH MARRIAGE IN THE SAME WAY THEY BUY A CAR.

a car. When you want to buy a new car, how do you go about it? You go to various car dealerships, compare the models and features, make your selection, sign the papers, and then drive your new car home. The mere act of getting married is like purchasing that new car; both are relatively simple to do. You look at the choices, find somebody you like, go to a minister or justice of the peace for the ceremony, receive your marriage certificate, and then go home with your new spouse.

At first, everything seems effortless. Buying a new car, driving it home, parking it in the garage, and admiring it in its mint condition isn't any problem. Driving with the full tank of gas that the car dealership gave you isn't any problem. Similarly, it's easy to marry a spouse, step over the threshold, and enjoy the honeymoon. Cruising on lovey-dovey honeymoon feelings is fine for a while.

However, buying a car is one thing; operating and maintaining it is something else. Likewise, getting married is one thing, while maintaining and growing in the relationship is another.

A car is meant to be a benefit to you, to help meet your transportation needs. However, you must understand the needs of the car, because there will come a time when that gas tank will need to be refilled. There will come a time when the car will need an oil change. There will come a time when repairs will need to be made. If you don't know the needs of a car, you will say, "What's wrong with this crazy car? Come on, car, you've been running for the last month. What is wrong with you?" All the time you are swearing at the car, the car is sitting there wanting to serve you. Yet it can't, because you don't know its needs and aren't attending to them.

WOULD YOU FEED A PLATE OF RIBS TO A PLANT?

Suppose you then say to yourself, "Well, when I get thirsty, I drink water, so the car must need water. I'm going to fill the gas tank with water." You try to attend to the needs of the car based on your own needs. Now you're in trouble, because the water you put in the gas tank has gone through the car's system and damaged it. Now your car won't run at all. So you say to your car, "When I drink water, I'm revived. What is wrong with you?" Your needs are not the same as your car's needs, and your car's needs are not the same as your needs. When you want a car or anything else to function, don't give it what you need. Find out what it needs, and then give it what it needs; then it will work for you.

What has been happening in relationships between males and females is that we have, in a sense, been putting water in the gas tank. We've been trying to function without understanding or addressing the other's individual needs. We have been trying to operate based only on what we need. That's why many relationships are at a standstill. That's why there has been so much misunderstanding and conflict between men and women throughout history.

We assume that a man needs what a woman needs and a woman needs what a man needs. In many ways, this is not the case. The differences are so great they will astound you. Suppose ribs are your favorite food. Can you imagine trying to feed a plant with a plateful of ribs? You enjoy ribs, but the plant can't take them in or digest them. To grow plants, you must understand that they need absorbable nutrients, water, and light. The same basic principle applies to men and women. There are certainly similarities between males and females, but each also has a unique design and unique needs. We must come to understand the purpose of all the elements related to the function and design of men and women. Otherwise, we will be continually frustrated in our relationships.

Moreover, because the nations of the world have tended to be governed by men, most societies have been set up to address the needs of the male before the needs of the female. To address the plight of the female and the conflict between men and women, we must learn, understand, and appreciate the woman's unique design. It is important for all people to understand the nature of the female as she was created in God's image and as she relates to the man.

This knowledge is not just for those who are in a marriage relationship. Whether you are married or single, male or female, young or old, you have interactions with women in the family, the workplace, the church, the government, and almost every other arena of life. If you don't understand how a woman is designed, you will not be able to deal honestly and effectively with her in these realms of life.

Of course, understanding the design of a woman (and a man) is also extremely important for a marriage relationship. When we learn what it truly means to be female and male, we can effectively enter into relationships with others, including the marriage relationship. If you are currently unmarried, you can learn who you are and why you are the way you are. You can discover how the opposite sex is designed and functions. Then, if you do marry, your marriage will be successful. You won't have many of the conflicts that arise out of ignorance of the purpose and value of women and men.

The needs of both males and females need to be learned. However, because the woman has been so misunderstood and devalued over the years, the focus of this book is on her design and needs; at the same time, it makes reference to how her makeup relates to the makeup of the man.

GOD'S PURPOSE

Nobody knows how something is supposed to function better than its maker. Can I suggest to you that the best way for us to make progress in the relationship between men and women is to go back to the beginning—to see what was in the mind and heart of the Creator when He made humanity? Knowing our original design and inherent makeup is the only way to bring about lasting, positive change in the way men and women interact with one another in all the realms of life.

> NOBODY KNOWS HOW SOMETHING IS MEANT TO FUNCTION BETTER THAN ITS MAKER.

I am persuaded that understanding and living in God's original purpose is crucial to restoring right relationships between men and women. Proverbs 19:21 summarizes this idea well: *"Many are the plans in a man's heart, but it is the Lord's purpose that prevails."* God is a God of purpose, and everything that He made in this life, including men and women, has a purpose. We can fight against His purpose, but if we do, we will be unfulfilled and frustrated. He made us the way we are for His purposes and for our benefit.

Throughout this book, we will continually come back to these two essential principles:

+ The purpose of something determines its nature (or design).
+ The nature (or design) of something determines its needs.

The nature of the woman must be understood in light of her purpose, and her needs must be understood in light of her nature. Otherwise, she will be unable to fulfill the purpose for which she was created.

The most important thing we can find out about ourselves and others is the purpose of our existence. The sad consequence of men and women misunderstanding each other is that, when purpose is not known, abuse is inevitable. We've had enough of that.

WHAT IS A WOMAN'S PLACE?

The controversy over the role, position, and rights of the woman over the years has often centered around these apparently competing views of what a woman's place is:

+ "A woman's place is in the home."

+ "A woman's place is in the world—in business, education, and government."

Both of these views fail to capture the essence of a woman's purpose and design.

Where, ultimately, is a woman's place? A woman's place is, before anything else, *in God*. (The same is true for a man.) It is in the way He created her, in the tremendous value He gives her, and in the pur-poses He has for her. Only when we grasp the implications of this truth will we resolve the controversy and conflict surrounding the role of the woman in the world.

> A WOMAN'S PLACE IS IN GOD.

PRINCIPLES

1. If you have to ask somebody for your rights, you are admitting that he or she has ownership of them.

2. A woman's position and rights are God-given and inherent.

3. The essential nature of women and men has been forgotten by the world.

4. Culture and tradition have passed along distorted views of humanity.

5. Most women have obtained their identities from men rather than from God.

6. The devaluing of women is preventing them from living in the fullness of God's purposes for them.

7. The way to make progress is to go back to God's original intent in creation.

8. The purpose of something determines its nature or design.

9. The nature of something determines its function and needs.

10. A woman's place is in God.

CHAPTER ONE STUDY QUESTIONS

QUESTIONS FOR REFLECTION

1. In what ways is it "a man's world" in the society or culture you live in? What do you think of this mind-set? How has this attitude affected you in your own life experience?

2. Name several traditional perceptions of women that still persist in the world today.

3. To what extent has your self-image or identity been formed by your family? Your culture? God?

EXPLORING GOD'S PRINCIPLES AND PURPOSES

4. Why do social and political advances on behalf of women not do enough to change negative societal attitudes toward women? (pp. 16–17)

5. Women's movements have traditionally approached the problem of the devaluing of women by demanding equal rights with men. Yet one of the principles given in chapter one is the following: "If you have to ask somebody for your rights, you are admitting that he or she has ownership of them." (pp. 18–19, 28) Do you agree or disagree with this statement? Why?

6. What do you consider a woman's rights? On what or whom do you base those rights?

7. Ultimately, what is the underlying cause of the devaluing of women? (p. 21)

8. Do you think women and men can be equal *and* different in their physical and emotional makeup? Why or why not?

9. What kinds of conflicts have you or those you know experienced with members of the opposite sex?

10. What happens when you seek to meet the needs of another person based on your own assessment of what he or she needs rather than considering that person's perspective?

11. These two essential principles are underlying themes of *Understanding the Purpose and Power of Women*:

    + The purpose of something determines its nature (or design).
    + The nature (or design) of something determines its needs.

    The nature of the woman must be understood in light of her purpose, and her needs must be understood in light of her nature. Otherwise, she will be unable to fulfill the purpose for which she was created. The most important thing women and men can find out about themselves and others is the purpose of their existence. (p. 26)

(a) What do you think is the purpose of your existence?

(b) How would you define God's purpose for your existence—as an individual and as a person with a God-given gender?

CONCLUSION

Where, ultimately, is a woman's place? A woman's place is, before anything else, *in God*. (The same is true for a man.) It is in the way He created her, in the tremendous value He gives her, and in the purposes He has for her.

Only when we grasp the implications of this truth will we resolve the controversy and conflict surrounding the role of the woman in the world. We will begin to discover these implications as we explore God's original intent in creation for both males and females in chapter two.

APPLYING GOD'S PRINCIPLES TO YOUR LIFE

THINKING IT OVER

+ Do you think there is a difference between the way you see yourself and the way God views you and the purposes He has for you? If so, are you willing to become all God has created you to be?

+ In what ways, if any, have you or women you know been hindered from personal growth and the development of gifts and talents because of negative attitudes or misunderstanding about women?

PRAYING ABOUT IT

+ Ask God to begin renewing your understanding of who He created the woman to be in her purpose, design, needs, and role.

+ If you are experiencing or have experienced conflicts with those of the opposite sex, ask God to reveal to you the true cause of these conflicts and how to respond to them based on His Word.

ACTING ON GOD'S TRUTH

+ If you have been hurt by society's or a particular person's devaluing of women, allow the grace of God to enter the situation by forgiving in Christ those who have wronged you and allowing Him to bring healing and even good out of the situation. (See Romans 8:28.)

The most important thing we can find out about ourselves and others is the purpose of our existence.

TWO

GOD'S PURPOSE IN CREATION

Many are the plans in a man's heart,
but it is the LORD's purpose that prevails.
—Proverbs 19:21

The source of so many of our problems in this world, including the misunderstanding and mistreatment of women, is that we have lost our understanding of what it means to be human as God created us. We have lost our sense of purpose. I am convinced that, in every country in the world, both men and women are suffering from this ignorance of purpose. The best thing for us to do is to discover and live in the original plan of the One who created humanity. Only then will we learn the inherent nature and rights of women and men, so that both female and male can live in freedom and fulfillment.

In the next chapter, we will discover a crucial aspect of God's original purpose for humanity—one that has been forgotten by most of the world for thousands of years. This purpose is key to our understanding of how God made men and women equal, unique, and complementary in design.

To gain the fullest understanding of this aspect of creation, however, we must first briefly consider the significance of what it means that we have been created *purposefully* by God. When we understand this concept, we will see how important it is for our well-being that we discover God's purposes for us.

SEVEN PRINCIPLES OF PURPOSE

The following seven principles of purpose will help us to understand God's original intent for us in creation.

1. God is a God of purpose.
2. God created everything with a purpose.

3. Not every purpose is known to us because we have lost our understanding of God's original intent for us.

4. Where purpose is not known, abuse is inevitable.

5. To discover the purpose of something, never ask the creation; ask the creator.

6. We find our purpose only in the mind of our Maker.

7. God's purpose is the key to our fulfillment.

GOD IS A GOD OF PURPOSE

God is a purposeful Being. He purposes, He plans, and then He carries out His plans. God always knew what He wanted to create before He made it; similarly, He always knows what He wants to carry out before He accomplishes it.

This theme is found throughout the Bible, which we can consider God's handbook for our lives. Here are various expressions of His purposeful nature:

And God said, "Let there be light," and there was light.

(Genesis 1:3)

But the plans of the LORD *stand firm forever, the purposes of his heart through all generations.* (Psalm 33:11)

The LORD *Almighty has sworn, "Surely, as I have planned, so it will be, and as I have purposed, so it will stand."* (Isaiah 14:24)

As the rain and the snow come down from heaven, and do not return to it without watering the earth and making it bud and flourish, so that it yields seed for the sower and bread for the eater, so is my word that goes out from my mouth: It will not return to me empty, but will accomplish what I desire and achieve the purpose for which I sent it.

(Isaiah 55:10–11)

God...has saved us and called us to a holy life—not because of anything we have done but because of his own purpose and grace. This grace was given us in Christ Jesus before the beginning of time.

(2 Timothy 1:8–9)

Men swear by someone greater than themselves, and the oath confirms what is said and puts an end to all argument. Because God wanted to make the unchanging nature of his purpose very clear to the heirs of what was promised, he confirmed it with an oath.

(Hebrews 6:16–17)

God is purposeful, and He always carries out His purposes. I want to direct your attention to Isaiah 14:24 and Hebrews 6:16–17, which illustrate a vital aspect of God's purposeful nature. First, the verse from Isaiah: *"The Lord Almighty has sworn, 'Surely, as I have planned, so it will be, and as I have purposed, so it will stand'"* (Isaiah 14:24).

The first part of the verse says that God has sworn an oath. Now, when people swear an oath, they have to find something higher than themselves by which to swear. *"Men swear by someone greater than themselves, and the oath confirms what is said and puts an end to all argument"* (Hebrews 6:16). We usually swear by the Bible or by some great institution. There is only one problem with God's swearing an oath: there is no one above Him. So God has to swear by Himself.

If you were called to be a witness in court, you would be asked to swear on the Bible, "I swear to tell the truth, the whole truth, and nothing but the truth, so help me, God." If you were to lie, it would be the same as desecrating the integrity of the Bible—and you would destroy your own integrity as well. If you break your vow, then whatever you swear by is desecrated or destroyed.

When God swears an oath regarding something, He has to fulfill what He swore to do, because He is totally faithful to Himself. God doesn't want us to have any doubt about this aspect of His nature. *"Because God wanted to make the unchanging nature of his purpose very clear to the heirs of what was promised, he confirmed it with an oath"* (Hebrews 6:17).

We see this principle expressed in the second part of Isaiah 14:24, which says,

> **BEFORE GOD'S PURPOSE WOULD CHANGE, HE WOULD CEASE BEING GOD.**

"*Surely, as I have planned, so it will be.*" God is saying, in effect, "When I swear to do something, before that plan fails, I would stop being God." The third part of the verse says, "*As I have purposed, so it will stand.*" Again, He is saying, "When I purpose to do something, and when I give something a purpose, before that purpose would change, I would stop being God." God isn't ever going to stop being God. So when He swears an oath regarding something, you can be certain that He is going to do what He has said.

If we look at the verses that follow Isaiah 14:24, we read,

> *This is the plan determined for the whole world; this is the hand stretched out over all nations. For the* LORD *Almighty has purposed, and who can thwart him* [stop, interfere with, or cancel His purpose]? *His hand is stretched out, and who can turn it back?*
>
> (Isaiah14:26–27)

In essence, God is saying, "My purpose will be accomplished. No one can interfere with it or hinder it. When I give a purpose to something, your plans, ideas, opinions, perceptions, and prejudices about what you think its purpose should be are inapplicable. What you think about what I have purposed is not going to change My purpose and design. And before My purpose could change, I would have to stop being God."

Let me ask you, If it comes to a contest between you and God, who do you think is going to win? If God sets a purpose for something, there isn't anything we can do to change it. "*Many are the plans in a man's heart, but it is the Lord's purpose that prevails*" (Proverbs 19:21). What we need to keep in mind, however, is that if we try to change His plans, we're working against ourselves, because He created us for good and has our best interests in mind.

That means that since God made the female and the male for certain purposes, and He designed them to fulfill those purposes, there isn't anything you and I can do to change them. We cannot alter His design. Psychology may try to tell us the purpose of women and men, but psychology cannot influence God's purposes and design; they are unchangeable. All psychology can do is investigate and explore the mysteries of the nature of women and men. Psychology can never change their nature. Theology may also try to tell us the purpose of humanity, but theology cannot influence God, either. What theology says about God and men is only as true as it accurately expresses their nature.

Theology is very limited if it is based on only what a person has experienced. A person should never build a doctrine based solely on his experience with God or what he perceives his experience to have been. Don't ever confuse your limited knowledge of God with biblical doctrine, because your knowledge may change next week. What you know about God today is what He has shown you so far. Tomorrow, you will know and understand more. The Bible is God's revelation of Himself to us, and it is our most reliable source of His nature and purposes.

GOD CREATED EVERYTHING WITH A PURPOSE

Let us now consider the nature of purpose itself. Purpose is the original intent of the creator in the creation of something. It is what is in the creator's mind that causes him to fashion his product in a certain manner. In short, purpose motivates the action of creation. This results in precision production.

Since God is a God of purpose, He never created anything hoping that it would turn out to be something viable. He first decided what it was to be, then He made it. This means that He always begins with a finished product in mind.

Consider these questions:

Why are humans different from animals?

Why is a bird different from a fish?

Why is the sun different from the moon?

Why does one star differ from another star?

Why are women different from men?

I want to answer these questions with a statement: Everything is the way it is because of *why* it was created, because of its purpose. The *why* dictates the design. God created everything with a purpose, and He created everything with the ability to fulfill its purpose. God's purposes were always planned out ahead of time; everything was al ready "made" in the mind of the Maker before He created it.

What this means is that God never gives a purpose to something after He has made it; rather, He *builds* everything to fulfill the specific purpose He already had in mind for it. God designed everything to function in its purpose, and everything is the way it is because its purpose requires it to be so. The purpose of a thing determines its nature, its design, and its features.

> **THE PURPOSE OF SOMETHING DETERMINES ITS NATURE, DESIGN, AND FEATURES.**

To understand how we function as human beings, we have to go to the Manual given to us by the Designer and Manufacturer who created us. First Corinthians 15:38 affirms the principle that God made everything according to its intended purpose: *"But God gives [a seed] a body as he has determined, and to each kind of seed he gives its own body."* Let's carefully consider this instruction from God's Manual. When it says, *"God gives [a seed] a body,"* this means that He designs this seed as He determines. Notice that He gives the seed a body *"as he has determined."* To determine means to make a decision before you start. So God determined what He wanted, and then He made it the way He wanted it to be.

"When you sow, you do not plant the body that will be, but just a seed, perhaps of wheat or of something else. But God...." (vv. 37–38). "But God." We're talking about God, Incorporated. He's the Manufacturer. He created everything. *"God gives it a body as he has determined, and to each kind of seed he gives its own body. All flesh is not the same"* (vv. 38–39). God said that *"all flesh is not the same."* Let's say it another way: all species are different. God determined that they would be different; therefore, they are different.

"Men have one kind of flesh, animals have another, birds another and fish another" (v. 39). Of course, the word *"flesh"* in this instance does not refer to meat; instead, it refers to the nature of the creature—its characteristic design. God determined that human beings would be different from animals in their nature. He also determined that birds and fish would have distinct natures. The passage goes on to say,

> There are also heavenly bodies and there are earthly bodies; but the splendor ["glory" NKJV] of the heavenly bodies is one kind, and the splendor ["glory" NKJV] of the earthly bodies is another. The sun has

one kind of splendor ["glory" NKJV], the moon another and the stars another; and star differs from star in splendor ["glory" NKJV].

(1 Corinthians 15:40–41)

The sun is meant to do a job that the moon isn't supposed to do, so God created the moon different from the sun. The moon is made to do its job, and no other job. The moon does not give light; it reflects light. Therefore, God did not put any light on the moon. God also made stars of different sizes and luminosity, for His own purposes. The point is that God made everything the way it is because of what it is supposed to do.

To further illustrate this principle, look at the clothes you are wearing. You will see that the designer and manufacturer created them with a purpose. The purpose was to produce a garment that you could wear to cover your body and to keep you either cool or warm. In order to fulfill this purpose, the designer had to fashion your clothes in such a way that they would do the job, and do it efficiently. Notice how your clothes fit your body. Your sleeves are not down to your feet. Your collar is not around your waist. Your clothes were designed for the purpose for which they were made. The same thing is true of other types of products.

There's another aspect of purpose and design that we need to consider. Suppose you buy a camera. Even though you may not understand everything about how your camera was made, its components

> WE HAVE DISREGARDED THE MANUAL AND THEN BECOME FRUSTRATED BECAUSE OUR RELATIONSHIPS AREN'T WORKING.

are still necessary for the fulfillment of its purpose. Just because you don't understand the nature of a product or can't operate it, you shouldn't get angry. There probably isn't anything wrong with it; you just don't know how it works. If you can't operate your camera, it doesn't mean that you should throw it away. You don't understand what was in the mind of those who made the camera, because that is their area of expertise. However, they are aware of that, so they provided a manual for you to refer to as you use your camera.

When it comes to male-female relationships, it is as if we have bought the camera without proper training on how to operate it. We have disregarded the Manual, and then we have become frustrated or angry because we haven't been able to get our relationships to work—usually after paying good money for them, too. When many people get married, they spend vast amounts of money on the wedding, but they don't know how a marriage is supposed to function.

Now, even though we have thrown away the Manual, we still often look around for help and advice. Many people turn to popular talk shows, magazines, and books to find out how to make their relationships work. However, many of these media dispense cheap psychology. Be careful when you start taking their advice on relationships, because half of the people on those programs and in those articles aren't married and never were, and they probably can't stay married if they are.

God is our Designer and Manufacturer. He knew exactly what He wanted when He thought of the female. He had her in mind before He made her. He first concluded what He wanted, then He created her and caused Her to function in exactly the way He had planned. He did the same thing with the male. He created him after He had finished deciding what the male was supposed to be. God did not venture out into the manufacturing business hoping He could create something that would work. He started out with an original design in mind, and His finished product parallels His intended purpose. He is the only One who knows how humanity is intended to successfully function.

NOT EVERY PURPOSE IS KNOWN TO US

So everything in life, everything that God has created, has a purpose and is designed according to that purpose. However, not every purpose is known to us. Humanity has lost its knowledge of God's purposes. It has not respected the fact that God's creation and His directions for living were established for a specific reason and that, if that purpose is abandoned, we will never function properly as human beings.

In chapter three, we will learn the extent of what transpired when humanity rejected God's plan. What we need to recognize at this point is that the result of this abandonment has been debilitating for us: we have grown further and further away from God's original intent and design, so that we function less and less as we were meant to. This has left us incomplete, frustrated, and in conflict with one another.

The first chapter of Romans explains that when people reject or are ignorant of the purposes of God, they end up continually abusing themselves. They abuse their bodies, their minds, their relationships, and their talents.

> *Although they knew God, they neither glorified him as God nor gave thanks to him, but their thinking became futile and their foolish hearts were darkened.* (Romans 1:21)

This verse describes those who did not know the purpose of God and did not even care to find out what it is. Even though they knew something about God and His ways, they did not want Him in their lives. They did not want to know what He wanted them to know. They were saying, in effect, "Keep Your opinions about who we are to Yourself, God. We know You made us, but mind Your own business. We know You're there, but leave us alone."

The next verse tells us the result of their decision: "*Although they claimed to be wise, they became fools*" (v. 22). They "*exchanged the truth of God for a lie*" and "*exchanged natural relations for unnatural ones*" (vv. 25–26).

When does the exchange of natural for unnatural take place? It takes place when purpose is either ignored or unknown. "*Furthermore, since they did not think it worthwhile to retain the knowledge of God, he gave them over to a depraved mind, to do what ought not to be done*" (v. 28). They did not think it worthwhile to find out God's purpose for the world or to retain the knowledge of God as to why He made humanity. They didn't check to find out why God made women and men. They didn't try to find out what God knows about the things He has made. They didn't want to know, so they relied on their own inclinations.

> HUMANITY HAS BEEN SAYING, "MIND YOUR OWN BUSINESS, GOD."

The above statements from Romans are a description of humanity as a whole. We have rejected knowing God and His purposes, and so God's original intent for us has not been communicated in many of our cultures and traditions. It has been lost or obscured. Instead, distorted views have been passed down, so that people do not know how to relate to one another as they were meant to. The problem is that, when we do not know how we are to function, we end up abusing one another.

WHERE PURPOSE IS UNKNOWN, ABUSE IS INEVITABLE

When humanity rejected God, He gave them what they wanted. He gave them over to their passions (Romans 1:24, 26). That's not as simple as it might sound. If God had just given us over to what we wanted, the implication might have been that we can succeed in spite of Him. But when God gave us over, He also allowed us to experience the inevitable results of our actions. God didn't just say, "Okay, go, carry on." He said, "If you carry on, you're going to end up depraved, because that isn't the way I made you" (v. 28).

The principle here is that you cannot move away from God and be successful. You cannot cut off your relationship with the Manufacturer and expect to find genuine parts somewhere else. When you ignore the warranty, any part you try to find on your own will not be genuine. You cannot develop into a better product without the help of the Manufacturer.

> YOU CANNOT MOVE AWAY FROM GOD'S PLAN AND BE SUCCESSFUL.

God says that when we reject His purposes, He gives us over to a depraved mind. In other words, He's telling us, "Without Me, your mind isn't going to get any better; it will only get worse." Therefore, if we think we can find out how to be better women or men without God, we are in trouble, for the consequences are serious. When we believe that we don't need God, we get worse and worse. How many people have been suffering from these very consequences? If you don't want to live in God's purpose for mankind, then you will end up doing yourself harm.

"*Many are the plans in a man's heart, but it is the* LORD's *purpose that prevails*" (Proverbs 19:21). We have many plans, but God has a purpose. Most of the time, our plans are not in harmony with God's purpose. I think it is appropriate to include the concept of opinions or perceptions in the word "*plans.*" We have many opinions and perceptions regarding what things should be like or what they are for, but God has a purpose for everything that He made. Therefore, what you think the purpose of something is, and what its purpose actually is, could be different. The problem is that, if your plans are not in keeping with God's purpose, then you will either suffer yourself or inflict abuse on others, because where purpose is not known, abuse is inevitable. If you don't know the purpose of a thing, all you will do is abuse it, no matter how sincere, committed, serious, or innocent you are.

We shouldn't attempt to use anything until we find out why it exists, because when we don't know what the maker intended for it, we will not treat his creation appropriately. We need to fully understand that where purpose is not known, abuse is inevitable. If you don't know what was in the mind of a maker of a thing, all you can do, at best, is not use it properly. However, usually you will go beyond that and abuse it. If you don't know the purpose for your existence, then no matter how earnest or sincere you are, all you can do is abuse your life. The most important thing for us to do, therefore, is to find out God's purpose for us. Unless we have this knowledge, we will abuse what He has created. We have been doing that with the woman for thousands of years.

What happens when we don't know the real reason and purpose for our existence?

> *The wrath of God is being revealed from heaven against all the godlessness and wickedness of men who suppress the truth by their wickedness, since what may be known about God is plain in them, because God has made it plain to them.*   (Romans 1:18–19)

The Scripture says that the wrath of God is already being revealed from heaven against ungodliness. I believe this statement means that when you turn away from God, you cause many of your own problems; God is not punishing you. Much of your hurt comes in the package of consequences you receive as a result of the decision you made to ignore God and His ways. The burning is in the heat. In other words, you don't need God's intervention to get burned; just put your hand into the fire. The judgment of putting your hand into the fire is inherent in the fire itself: you get burned.

Here is another illustration of this principle. The judgment for drinking poison is death from poisoning. You don't need God to kill you after you drink poison. What this statement is saying is that God doesn't have to do anything to judge you. You judge yourself by your activities, by your participation based on your decision to live according to your own knowledge. Consequently, you are a victim of your own decision, not of God's judgment.

Some people blame the devil for the results of their actions. Don't blame the devil; he just takes advantage of your decisions. The devil cannot dominate you or force you to do anything. The devil waits for your decisions. When you make a bad one, he'll ride it to the end, or just as far as he can, and he'll try to bring you down with it. Satan is not the culprit. The culprit is your rejection or ignorance of God's purpose. You don't know God's purpose for living, and so you abuse your life. Be careful; that abuse can cripple or kill you.

Even though humanity has turned away from God, He still creates us with gifts and talents that are intended to be used to fulfill His purposes. Yet since we don't know how they are to be used, we take the talents He has given us and use them against ourselves and others.

WE OFTEN USE GOD'S GIFTS TO HURT OTHERS RATHER THAN TO BLESS THEM.

For example, Romans 1:29 says that one of the manifestations of a depraved mind is unrighteousness or wickedness. Some of the wickedest people in the world are wise when it comes to information. They are sharp people. They're so sharp, they can be wicked with class. Some people are gifted, but they use their gift in such a wicked way that their victims don't know what hits them until it's all over.

Wickedness, greed, and all kinds of depravity can be combined with intelligence and skill, and be used for evil purposes. For example, it takes talent to be envious in a truly effective way. Some people hate you, but you don't know it because they're so good at it. They keep you from being successful in your job through well-placed memos to your superiors. If they could just use that energy and talent for good purposes, they could uplift people instead of bringing them down. They abuse the very thing that was given to them to be a blessing to others. When purpose is not known, abuse is inevitable.

Some of us are excellent at murder. Murder does not just mean stabbing someone with a knife. Jesus said that if you hate someone, it is the equivalent of murder. (See Matthew 5:21–22.) Some people haven't acted on their feelings, but they have mentally wished for another's death.

Slander is another example of this type of murder. We can use the talent of verbal eloquence to assassinate another's character with style. Slander doesn't necessarily mean lying about someone else; it can mean twisting the truth with the intent to hurt. It takes talent to do that. When some people want to get back at others, they stand up in public arenas and use their mouths as guns and their words as bullets. When they finish shooting, their victims are dead, and everybody knows it. Some of their victims never resurrect from these attacks.

A third example of this type of murder is gossip. We all probably have met some excellent, qualified gossips. They train in it. They know how to give you just enough to create a tempting aroma. If some people would take the energy with which they gossip and use it for promoting the Gospel, the world would be changed.

The skill and talent necessary to carry out some of this behavior comes from God, but it has been perverted because it is not being used for God's purposes. When purpose is not known, abuse is inevitable.

The apostle Paul told us that everything God made is available to us to do with what we want, yet he added a warning: *"Everything is permissible for me'—but not everything is beneficial. 'Everything is permissible for me'—but I will not be mastered by anything'"* (1 Corinthians 6:12). Then he gave an example. He said, *"Food for the stomach and the stomach for food'"* (v. 13). What was he talking about? He was saying that there is a purpose for everything, but if you don't know the purpose of something, it can enslave you. Not everything is beneficial.

Paul was implying that if we are to use food in a way that is beneficial to us, we must understand both the purpose of the stomach and the purpose of food. The stomach and food were made for one another. God designed the stomach for food and food for the stomach so that we could receive nutrition to sustain our physical lives. Yet we can abuse the relationship between the stomach and food by overeating or by eating food that has no nutritional value. This can cause us to become overweight or lack proper nutrition, resulting in a variety of health problems. When purpose is not known, or when desire prompts us to misuse purpose, abuse is inevitable.

Paul was saying that you can use anything you want, but you had better find out what its purpose is if you want it to benefit you. If you don't understand the purpose of something, it can become like a curse to you. For instance, some single people become nervous and depressed that they're getting older, and so they marry the first person who comes along. They are permitted to marry. They are of age. It is permissible—but will it be beneficial to them? The criteria for marriage is not merely being old enough, but whether or not it will be beneficial. If you don't have a clear understanding of the purpose of something, it's not going to benefit you. That is the reason the divorce rate is so high. When purpose is not known, abuse is inevitable.

These illustrations emphasize what happens when we don't know God's purposes: we end up hurting ourselves or hurting others. Sometimes we do so out of ignorance, but at other times we do so knowingly. At times, to assuage our guilt, we even encourage others to continue such abuse. Romans 1:32 says, "*Although they know God's righteous decree* [they know what He says in His Word] *that those who do such things deserve death, they not only continue to do these very things but also approve of those who practice them.*"

They know what is written in God's Word—that those who do wicked things deserve death. (See verses 29–32.) Yet they not only continue to do those things, but they also encourage others in them. When a person is wrong, he feels better if someone else keeps him company in his wrongdoing. If I'm messing up but you're not messing up, then I *really* feel messed up. However, if I'm messing up and I tangle you up in my mess, then we can both feel justified in our actions.

A person who is willfully ignorant of the purposes of God generally doesn't want anyone else to know them, either. Jesus told the Pharisees, the religious leaders of His day, that this is essentially what they were doing. Many of them knew the truth but refused to accept it. "*Woe to you, teachers of the law and Pharisees, you hypocrites! You shut the kingdom of heaven in* men's faces. *You yourselves do not enter, nor will you let those enter who are trying to*" (Matthew 23:13).

If we ignore or don't know God's purposes for us, we are in danger of hurting ourselves and others. When purpose is not known, or is rejected, abuse is inevitable.

TO DISCOVER PURPOSE, NEVER ASK THE CREATION; ASK THE CREATOR

Again, nobody knows a product and how it should work better than the one who made it. In the same way, the one who created the product is the best one to fix it when it has become marred. When a potter works on a pot and sees that it has a flaw in it, the potter either remolds the clay and starts over, or if the pot already has been fired in an oven, the potter has to smash it and start over.

Now, when the clay starts talking back to the potter, something is wrong. (See Isaiah 29:16.) The potter knows better than the pot how the pot should be fashioned. The pot can't say to the potter, "You shouldn't have made me this way," because the pot can't see the whole picture, the way the potter can. When it comes to the relationship between males and females and society's devaluation of women, we have too often murmured against the Potter rather than trying to understand how and why we were created. Moreover, our substitutes for His master design are flawed. Some of us need to have our attitudes, perspectives, and lives remolded. A few of us have gone so far in the wrong direction that we may need a total overhaul. That is why the principles in this book are very serious and very awesome, but also very necessary for the restoration of humanity to God's purposes.

So if you want to discover the purpose of something, never ask the creation; ask the one who made it. The creation might not think it has any worth, but the creator knows what it is made of. Many people do not think they have any worth or purpose.

> THE CREATION MAY NOT FEEL IT HAS WORTH, BUT THE CREATOR KNOWS WHAT IT IS MADE OF.

Yet the first chapter of our Manual tells us, "*God saw all that he had made, and it was very good*" (Genesis 1:31). There is something good in God's creation, no matter how confused it looks to us. There is something good about every person, even though it may be hard to find. There is something good about everything God has made. We need to go to Him to find the good purposes for which He has made us. *"For it is God who works in you to will and to act according to his good purpose"* (Philippians 2:13).

WE FIND OUR PURPOSE ONLY IN OUR MAKER

When we try to mend our relationships or change society using our own methods, we never totally succeed, and we often utterly fail. We fail because we are trying to bring about change for the wrong reasons and using the wrong methods. That is why we need to go back to the Manufacturer and receive His instructions for our lives. The only way for us to succeed is to discover and live in the purposes of our Maker, by undergoing a transformation in the way we think about ourselves as human beings.

Romans 12:1–2 encourages us to give ourselves to God so that we may receive His principles for living rather than conforming to this world's pattern of living.

> *Offer your bodies as living sacrifices, holy and pleasing to God—this is your spiritual act of worship. Do not conform any longer to the pattern of this world, but be transformed by the renewing of your mind. Then you will be able to test and approve what God's will is—his good, pleasing and perfect will.*

In other words, we are not to conform to this world's opinions of humanity's purpose but be transformed into God's original intent in creation, so that we can live in peace with ourselves and others. We do this by presenting our bodies to God, so they can line up with His purpose for our bodies, and by presenting our minds to Him, so they can line up with His purpose for our minds. Our minds are to be transformed as they are renewed. Then we will truly be able to know *"what God's will is—his good, pleasing and perfect will."*

Many of us don't know God's perfect purpose for our bodies. We've been abusing them—selling them cheaply, filling them with alcohol, drugs, nicotine, or too much food. We've been making a mess of our lives.

Our bodies are meant to be God's temple. When you present your body to the Manufacturer, what does He do with it? He fills it with His own Spirit, so you can be filled with His life and purpose. *"Do you not know that your body is a temple of the Holy Spirit, who is in you, whom you have received from God? You are not your own"* (1 Corinthians 6:19).

When you present your spirit to the Manufacturer, it becomes *"the candle of the Lord"* (Proverbs 20:27 KJV), an expression of the light of God. It is the same way when you present your mind and soul to your Maker. They are renewed by His Word, which is a light for your path (Psalm 119:105). David said in Psalm 19:7, *"The law of the LORD is perfect, converting the soul; the testimony of the LORD is sure, making wise the simple"* (NKJV). God's ways will transform your spirit, your mind, and your outlook. When you present yourself to God and learn from Him, you will understand His purpose.

Therefore, in order to pursue God's purpose, you first must present yourself to God, so that you can *know* His perfect will. Then you will be transformed, so that you can *do* His perfect will. In this way, His good purposes will be fulfilled in you.

GOD'S PURPOSE IS THE KEY TO OUR FULFILLMENT

Since everything God created was intentional, we can conclude that the female, as well as the male, was created intentionally. God didn't wonder why He made the woman or what her purpose should be after He created her. He was very clear about why He made this wonderful creation, and therefore we don't have to guess about her, either. The female was created to help fulfill God's eternal purpose. His eternal purpose is great, and within His larger purpose, He has many smaller purposes. Both the female and the male are to discover their individual purposes, which are part of God's larger plan.

Proverbs 19:21 is our foundational Scripture for understanding our true purpose as human beings: *"Many are the plans in a man's heart, but it is the LORD's purpose that prevails."* The key thoughts we're addressing here are that God has a purpose for everything, and that He will always accomplish His purpose in the end. The best way to experience fulfillment in your life is to find God's purpose and then work with Him to fulfill it.

In order for the woman truly to fulfill her purpose, she has to understand the purpose of God for humanity. In order for the man truly to fulfill his purpose, he has to understand the purpose of God for humanity. *"Therefore, I urge you, brothers, in view of God's mercy, to offer your bodies as living sacrifices, holy and pleasing to God—this is your spiritual act of worship"* (Romans 12:1). Becoming what He has purposed for us is an act of worship to our Creator.

GOD'S IDEAL PURPOSES

The seven principles of purpose in this chapter clearly show that if we do not know why the female was made, she will be misused or abused. In the chapters that follow, we will learn the purpose, nature, and design of the woman as she was created in the image of God and as she relates to the man. These are God's ideal purposes for women and men, which we desire to move toward. However, we must keep in mind that entering into God's purposes will be a continual process of learning and transformation. Therefore, we need to be patient with ourselves. We are starting where we are now—not at the place we should be, and not at the place at which we will arrive.

> WE SHOULD NEVER ACCEPT WHAT WE CURRENTLY HAVE AS THE NORM.

Paul told us, in regard to our spiritual growth, that we are to forget the things that are behind us and reach for what is ahead of us. We are to press on to the mark, which is the *"high calling of God in Christ Jesus"* (Philippians 3:14 KJV). When Jesus came to earth, He showed us the mark that we are to hit. So whatever He says is what we're supposed to pursue. He showed us God's original plan so that we could have something to aim at. We should never accept what we currently have as the norm. Even though it may be the current trend, if it's not what God intended, it's abnormal. We should never live so below our privilege that we begin to believe a lie and call it truth.

When you begin to understand and live in the purposes of God, people may become very uncomfortable with you. When you tell them, "Look, I know what it is to be a woman. I went to the Manufacturer and got the right Manual," they may say, "Oh, no, that's an old manual; it's out of date." However, we cannot improve on the original.

When we—both women and men—gain an understanding of our uniqueness and purpose in God, we will be able to assist one another in properly understanding and fulfilling the lives God created us to live. We will then also be able to live in right relationship with God, and in the freedom and blessings He planned for us in creation. What's more, when we mend the broken relationships between female and male, both of whom are created in the image of God, we will begin to see healing and new purpose for the individuals, communities, and nations of our world.

PRINCIPLES

1. God is a God of purpose.

2. When God swears an oath regarding something, He has to fulfill what He swore to do, because He is totally faithful to Himself.

3. God created everything according to its intended purpose.

4. Not every purpose is known to us because we have lost our understanding of God's original intent for us.

5. Where purpose is not known, abuse is inevitable.

6. You cannot move away from God's plan and be successful.

7. If you want to know the purpose of something, never ask the thing itself; ask the one who made it.

8. We find our purpose in the mind of our Maker.

9. God's purpose is the key to our fulfillment.

CHAPTER TWO STUDY QUESTIONS

QUESTIONS FOR REFLECTION

1. Do you feel you are fulfilling your purpose in life? In what ways are you using your God-given skills and talents to achieve that purpose?

EXPLORING GOD'S PRINCIPLES AND PURPOSES

2. List the seven principles of purpose: (pp. 33–34)

3. Can anyone interfere with or hinder God's purposes? Why or why not? (pp. 34–36)

4. What happens when we try to go against God's purposes for males and females? (p. 36)

5. God not only created everything with a purpose, but He also created everything with the ability to fulfill its purpose. Everything is the way it is because its purpose requires it to be so. (pp. 37–38) In light of this truth, complete the following:

   The purpose of a thing determines its _____, its _____, and its _____. (p. 38)

6. What happens when people reject or are ignorant of the purposes of God? (pp. 40–41)

7. God's ways will transform your spirit, your mind, and your outlook. When you present yourself to God and learn from Him, you will understand His purpose and be able to do His perfect will. In light of this truth, answer the following questions:

(a) When you present your body to your Maker, what happens? (pp. 48–49)

(b) When you present your spirit to your Maker, what does it become? (p. 49)

(c) When you present your mind and soul to your Maker, what is the result? (p. 49)

8. The female, as well as the male, was created _____. She was created to help fulfill God's _____ _____. (p. 49)

9. Becoming what God has purposed for us is an act of _____ to our Creator. (p. 50)

CONCLUSION

Gaining an understanding of mankind's uniqueness and purpose in God will not only enable us to fulfill our own purpose, but will also help us to assist others in knowing and fulfilling their purpose. Once we are in right relationship to God, we can mend broken relationships between women and men, both of whom are created in the image of God. In this way, we will begin to see healing and new purpose for the individuals, communities, and nations of our world.

APPLYING GOD'S PRINCIPLES TO YOUR LIFE

THINKING IT OVER

+ Think about your gifts and talents. Do you know the purpose for which God gave them to you? Have you used them to help or hinder others? Have you committed them to God, or do you do use them to promote yourself alone?

+ Entering into God's purposes is a continual process of learning and transformation. Therefore, we need to be patient with ourselves during this process. We are starting where we are now—not at the place we should be, and not at the place at which we will arrive. However, we should never accept what we currently have as the norm. Even though it may be the current trend, if it's not what God intended, it's abnormal. Are you doing as Philippians 3:13–14 suggests: *"One thing I do: Forgetting what is behind and straining toward what is ahead, I press on toward the goal to win the prize for which God has called me heavenward in Christ Jesus"*?

PRAYING ABOUT IT

+ Romans 12:1–2 encourages us to give ourselves to God so that we may receive His principles for living rather than conforming to this world's pattern of living. We are not to conform to the world's opinions of humanity's purpose but be transformed into God's original intent in creation. Have you been conforming to the world's ways of thinking and living in regard to your purpose? Commit yourself—spirit, mind, and body—to God and ask Him to transform your life so that it is renewed in His ways and purposes.

ACTING ON GOD'S TRUTH

+ Many people do not think they have much worth or purpose. Yet Genesis 1:31 says, *"God saw all that he had made, and it was very good."* There is something good in God's creation, no matter how confused it looks to us. There is something good about every person, even though it may be hard to find. Ask God to increase your ability to discern His goodness in others.

✦ Read Philippians 2:13: *"For it is God who works in you to will and to act according to his good purpose."* Make a decision to trust God fully that He is at work in your life through Christ and will enable you to fulfill the purposes He has for you.

Becoming what God has purposed for us is
an act of worship to our Creator.

THREE

THE PURPOSE AND NATURE OF HUMANITY

So God created man in his own image, in the image of God he created him; male and female he created them.
—Genesis 1:27

Let us now look at the purpose of humanity, starting with the first two human beings God created, because they represent all of us. When God created humanity, He had two overarching purposes in mind: *relation* and *vocation*. The first purpose is God's personal reason for creating us— for relationship with Himself. The second is His executive reason for creating us—for the lifework He designed us to carry out for Him in the earth.

THE CREATION OF MAN

The book of Genesis tells us of the origin of humanity. Genesis 1 is a declaration chapter. It declares what God did in creation. Genesis 2 is an explanation chapter. It explains how God accomplished His act of creation. In Genesis 1:26–27, we read,

> *Then God said, "Let Us make man in Our image, according to Our likeness; let them have dominion over...all the earth...." So God created man in His own image; in the image of God He created him; male and female He created them.* (NKJV)

The first question we need to ask is, Why did God decide to create man? The second is, What does it mean to be created in God's image? Third, What does it mean for man to have dominion over all the earth? Fourth, Why did God create male and female?

WHY DID GOD CREATE MAN?

The ultimate purpose behind the creation of man was—and is—love. The Scripture tells us that *"God is love"* (1 John 4:8, 16). What I especially like about this statement is that God doesn't just give love, He doesn't just show love, He **is** love. He desires to share His love with us because love is His essential quality.

> GOD CREATED MAN OUT OF LOVE.

From front to back, the Word of God teaches that God is love. Consider these passages:

> *The LORD appeared to us in the past, saying: "I have loved you with an everlasting love; I have drawn you with loving-kindness."*
> (Jeremiah 31:3)

> *The LORD your God is with you, he is mighty to save. He will take great delight in you, he will quiet you with his love, he will rejoice over you with singing.* (Zephaniah 3:17)

> *I am convinced that neither death nor life,…nor anything else in all creation, will be able to separate us from the love of God that is in Christ Jesus our Lord.* (Romans 8:38–39)

> *Because of his great love for us, God, who is rich in mercy, made us alive with Christ.* (Ephesians 2:4–5)

> *How great is the love the Father has lavished on us, that we should be called children of God!* (1 John 3:1)

God has many other qualities besides love that we could list. He is righteous, holy, omnipotent, almighty. He is all of these wonderful things. Yet God could be all of these attributes and still exist by Himself in isolation. He doesn't need anyone else in order to be holy. He doesn't need anyone else to be righteous. He doesn't need anyone to be almighty. He can be omnipotent, omnipresent, and all the rest of His qualities by Himself. However, it is the nature of love to give of itself, and it cannot give in isolation. In order for love to be fulfilled, it has to have someone to love, and it has to give to its beloved.

"I am the LORD, *and there is no other; apart from me there is no God"* (Isaiah 45:5). There is no other God besides the Lord, yet He is a God of relationship, not isolation. He desires someone of His nature and likeness whom He can love. Therefore, God's primary motivation in the creation of man was love. He created man because He wanted to share His love with a being like Himself, a being created in His image.

This truth is amazing to me. Genesis tells us that God created the heavens and the earth. He created all the plants and animals. He made the sun, the stars, the galaxies, the millennia, and the eons. He looked at all these remarkable things that He had created, and He said that they were good. However, He couldn't truly love these things because they were not like Him. Yes, they reflected His power, glory, and creativity; they revealed His nature and qualities, but they were not made in His essential likeness. It is man whom God created in His image to love.

In the New Testament, Jesus both affirms and exemplifies God's love for us. He said, *"For God so loved the world that He gave His only begotten Son"* (John 3:16 NKJV). *"He gave."* He gave because He loved. You cannot love without giving. When you love, you give. It's automatic. Yet in order to give love in a way that is truly fulfilling, the receiver has to be like the giver in nature; otherwise, the love would not be complete. You cannot give in a meaningful way to something that is not like you, because it cannot receive your gift in a way that will satisfy your giving. Giving is only complete when the receiver and the giver are alike. God desired a shared and mutual love—not a one-sided love.

God looked at what He had created, and here was this man, this beautiful duplicate of Himself. Here was someone to fulfill His love. This relationship of love was the primary purpose that God created man. This is not an abstract concept. This means that the entire human race—including you and me—were created by God to be loved by Him.

Some years ago, I was pondering the question of why, when humanity rejected God's ways, God didn't start over and make a new race of men. The reason is that God is not a two-timer. His love is pure and unconditional; it is not based on the actions of the receiver. Therefore, when we offer our lives to God, we should not do so believing that God merely feels sorry for us. We should go to God because, in response to such unconditional love, we can't love anyone else the way we love God.

God and humanity were made for one another. It doesn't matter whom else you love, you aren't ever going to be satisfied until you love God. No matter how many relationships you have and how many gifts you buy for others, when it's all over, you will still be lonely. Why? It is because the Person whom you were made to love above all else—God—doesn't have the place in your life that He needs to have. You were made to love God. Your love was designed to be fulfilled in Him.

WHAT DOES IT MEAN TO BE CREATED IN GOD'S IMAGE?

What is this image of God in which we were created?

GOD DREW MAN OUT OF HIMSELF.

When God said, *"Let us make man in our image, in our likeness"* (Genesis 1:26), He was saying, in effect, "Let Us make someone to love, and call it 'man.' Since We want man to be the object of Our love, We're going to make man in Our own image and in Our own likeness. This creation will be just like Us." Therefore, when God made man, He essentially drew man out of Himself, so that the essence of man would be just like Him. In this way, the receiver could be just like the Giver, and could reciprocate His love. God created man out of His own essence. Since *"God is spirit"* (John 4:24), He created man as spirit. This is a vital aspect of creation that we will return to again.

Man is the only being on the face of the planet—and even in the universe, that we know of—that is created in God's image. This includes angels. Nowhere in the Bible do you find that the angels are made in God's image. However, man came out of God and was created in His image and likeness. Man is the only being of God's creation that is like Him.

So man—the spirit-man—was created as a result of God's love. Note carefully that, at this point, we are still talking about the creation of man, the spirit. We are not yet talking about male and female. Whom did God create in His image? Man. Man is spirit, and spirits have no gender. The Bible never talks about a male or female spirit. God created the spirit-man without a gender.

Yet we next read in Genesis 1:27, *"God created man in his own image, in the image of God he created him; male and female he created them."* God took this spirit-man, and He placed him in two physical forms: male and female. The spirit-man is neither male nor female. However, to fulfill His eternal purposes, God used two physical forms, called male and female, to express the one entity of man. Therefore, the essence of both male and female is the resident spirit within them, called "man."

In the Bible, when God speaks to humanity, He uses the term *man*. He doesn't address the male or the female unless He's talking to individuals. Instead, He talks to the man within them both. He addresses the spirit-man. Many

THERE'S A MAN WITHIN THE WOMAN.

of us are preoccupied by the outward manifestation of male or female, when we should be focusing on the spirit-man. For example, some people say, "I don't believe in women preachers." However, they fail to realize that there's a man within the woman. If you don't like women preachers, then close your eyes and listen, because there's a man within her. Let the man within her preach. God deals with the inner being (Ephesians 3:16). Paul said in Galatians 3:28 that in the body of Christ there is neither male nor female, neither slave nor master. When God deals with people, He deals with their spirits.

Genesis 5:1–2 says, *"When God created man, he made him in the likeness of God. He created them male and female and blessed them. And when they were created, he called them* [together] *'man.'"* Whom did God call man? Both male and female. Therefore, it would be incorrect for you to call me "man" and to call my wife a "non-man." Both of us are man. God is referring to the spirit inside.

God deals with the man inside us because *"God is spirit, and his worshipers must worship in spirit and in truth"* (John 4:24). We worship God with our spirits, not with our gender. That means, if you are a man, before God, your spirit does not depend upon your wife. If you are a woman, before God, your spirit does not depend on your husband.

Many men seem to have this impression. They drop their wives off at church because they believe their wives are going to cover for them while they go off to some other activity. "She's the spiritual one in the house," they think. "She'll pray for the kids, and she'll pray for me. I'll just go and play baseball." Yet the man within the male and the man within the female are each responsible to God.

Many women misunderstand this truth, also. They seem to be waiting for their husbands to become Christians before they will worship God. If their husbands don't care about God, that fact has nothing to do with their own worship of Him. A woman has a spirit; she is a responsible spiritual being. Even if a woman's husband wants to live in an evil way and be an abomination to God, she is to worship the Lord anyway. God is not going to say to her, "Well, since your husband didn't worship Me, it's fine that you didn't, either."

The Bible says that every person must stand on his own feet before God. (See Romans 14:10.) God is going to deal with us Spirit to spirit. Therefore, spiritually, God does not care whether you are male or female. He is concerned with the spirit-man. Your relationship to God is not dependent on whether you are a male or a female. You must come to God through your spirit.

"MAN" MEANS BOTH MALE AND FEMALE. The presence of the spirit-man within us is why the Bible says that all men have sinned, rather than that "men and women have sinned." *"Death came to all men, because all sinned"* (Romans 5:12). The word *"men"* in this verse is translated from the Greek word *anthropos*, meaning human beings. With the exception of Jesus Christ, every human spirit-being from Adam forward has sinned, whether male or female. Have you ever wondered why, when a wife becomes a Christian, God doesn't always save her husband at the same time? The reason is that he's a different spirit-being altogether. God does say that believing spouses sanctify their unbelieving spouses, which means that they keep them in a protective environment so that God can reach them. (See 1 Corinthians 7:13–14.) However, these spouses still have to go to God of their own accord.

So the person who lives inside you, the real you, is the spirit-man. No matter what anybody else does, you are responsible for your relationship with God.

The fact that the same spirit of man resides in both female and male has generally been forgotten by humanity, so that men and women end up battling one another for supremacy, as if one needs to prove superiority over the other. Yet neither is superior, for they are both of the same essence, even with their differences.

WHAT DOES IT MEAN FOR MAN TO HAVE DOMINION?

The personal reason that God created humanity, therefore, was to establish a relationship of love with man. God created man—the spirit-man—in His own image, so that love could be freely given and received between Creator and created. God also created man for vocation—to carry out His purposes in the earth. What is the central nature of that purpose?

> *Then God said, "Let us make man in our image, in our likeness, and let them rule* ["have dominion" NKJV] *over the fish of the sea and the birds of the air, over the livestock, over all the earth, and over all the creatures that move along the ground." So God created man in his own image, in the image of God he created him; male and female he created them. God blessed them and said to them, "Be fruitful and increase in number; fill the earth and subdue it. Rule over the fish of the sea and the birds of the air and over every living creature that moves on the ground."* (Genesis 1:26–28)

Man was created to have dominion over the earth, to rule over it. Let us keep in mind that the word *"man"* in Genesis 1:26 refers to the species that God made, the spirit-being called "man." This means that the purpose of dominion was given to both male and female, since the spirit-man resides in each. Therefore, spiritually, both male and female have the same responsibility toward the earth.

What does it mean for man to have dominion over the world? First, God has entrusted the earth to the care of man. God's charge to humanity to have dominion means that man is to be the proprietor of the physical earth, including all the other living things in the world—fish, birds, livestock, all the animals. In Genesis 2, we read that the man was placed in the Garden of Eden to tend it and cultivate it. This is what mankind is to do with the entire earth: both tend it and cultivate it. God told humanity, in effect, "Rule over My world. Take care of it. Subdue it and fashion it with your own creativity." In this way, man would reflect the loving and creative spirit with which he was made in the image of God.

Yet having dominion means even more than taking care of the physical world. Since man is both physical and spiritual in nature, humanity is to reflect God and His purposes in the spiritual realm as well as in the earthly realm. Ephesians 3:10–11 tells us that God's eternal purpose for humanity was made possible through the coming of Christ:

> *His intent was that now, through the church, the manifold wisdom of God should be made known to the rulers and authorities in the heavenly realms, according to his eternal purpose which he accomplished in Christ Jesus our Lord.* (Ephesians 3:10–11)

God's eternal purpose is that the entire spiritual world, including the powers of darkness, will know His wisdom through us. What an awesome responsibility! If the rulers and authorities in the heavenly realms want to know what God is like and what He has accomplished, they are supposed to look at us. If the devil wants to know what God is like, he's supposed to look at us. Most of us aren't showing the devil what God is like; we're showing the devil what he is like. However, God's purpose is that He might display His manifold wisdom to all of the spirit world through those whom He has both created and redeemed in Christ. In this way, through the physical and spiritual realms, it has been given to man to reflect God's wisdom, creativity, power, and glory. Humanity is to reflect the attributes of the Creator, in whose image we were created.

WHY DID GOD MAKE MALE AND FEMALE?

Again, it is important to remember that this charge to have dominion was given to man. Let us look again at Genesis 5:1–2: "*When God created man, he made him in the likeness of God. He created them male and female and blessed them. And when they were created, he called them 'man.'*" "Man" is the name of the species God made. How, then, did God go about creating male and female, and why did He create them?

God took man and placed him in two separate physical "houses" so that He could fulfill His purposes for humanity and for the world. Therefore, although spirits have no gender, the houses in which they live do. The first house God made was the male; the second house God made was the female.

Genesis 1:26–27 implies that the process through which God created man as a spiritual being was different from the process through which God formed the male and female bodies. We can think of the distinction in this way: God

GOD CREATED MAN, BUT HE MADE MALE AND FEMALE.

created man, but He *made* male and female. The word *"make"* in verse 26 (*"Let us make man"*) and *"created"* in verse 27 (*"So God created man"*) are different Hebrew words. The word *"make"* is *asah*, and it means to form out of something that is already there. The word *"created"* is *bara*, which means to form out of nothing. These verses indicate that God *created* man in His own spiritual image, but that God also *made* man with a physical body. God used both of these words in reference to how He brought the first human being into existence. In effect, He was saying, "I will both create him and make him. I will create him out of nothing, and I will make him out of something."

God created the spiritual aspect of human beings out of His own being rather than out of anything from the physical world. The spirit of the first human was not created from matter; it came out of God's Spirit. God created the essential nature of man to be spirit, as He Himself is Spirit. (See John 4:24.) God just spoke the spirit of man into existence, similar to the way in which He spoke, *"'Let there be light,' and there was light"* (Genesis 1:3). Yet when God made the physical bodies of both male and female, He used material from the physical world that He had already created.

CREATION OF THE MALE

When God gave the spirit-man dominion over a physical earth, he gave him a physical body so that he could live and function in the world and rule over it. *"The Lord God formed the man from the dust of the ground and breathed into his nostrils the breath of life, and the man became a living being"* (Genesis 2:7). God formed a house from the dust of the ground; this house was the male. Then God housed the spirit-man in the male. Therefore, part of the male was created out of God's Spirit and part of the male was made out of dust, out of the dirt of the ground. God took what He had created (the spirit-man) and put it inside what He had made (the man's body). Then He placed the male in the Garden of Eden so that the man could rule what God had already created (the earth) through what God had made (the man). "*Now the* LORD *God had planted a garden in the east, in Eden; and there he put the man he had formed....The* LORD *God took the man and put him in the Garden of Eden to work it and take care of it*" (Genesis 2:8, 15).

CREATION OF THE FEMALE

In Genesis 2:7–17, we see that, at first, only the spirit in the male (let's call him the male-man) is ruling in the Garden. If God created man for the purpose of having a relationship of love, and then placed him in the male so that he could carry out his dominion over the world, what motivated God to make the female?

When God placed the spirit called "man" in the male, God and man could still give and receive love through their spirits. However, because the man now had a physical body, he also needed someone with whom to share human and physical love. This is a reflection of man's creation in the image of God. God is love. Man came from love and is made up of love, and love cannot dwell alone.

"*The* LORD *God said, 'It is not good for the man to be alone. I will make a helper suitable for him'*" (Genesis 2:18). Do you sense the implication of that verse? Even though the spirit within the male had communion with God, the male needed love. Genesis 2:19–20 tells us,

> Now the LORD *God had formed out of the ground all the beasts of the field and all the birds of the air. He brought them to the man to see what he would name them; and whatever the man called each living creature, that was its name. So the man gave names to all the livestock, the birds of the air and all the beasts of the field. But for Adam no suitable helper was found.*

The male-man had a problem. God told him, "You have the animals, but they aren't like you." Animals were created for man's enjoyment, and although they can give us some comfort, they cannot truly fulfill a person's need for love. Some people know that they need the love of other humans, but they are not brave enough to pursue it. They don't have the capacity to put aside their pride or their fears so they can risk love with another human being. Therefore, they turn to animals for companionship. You see, a dog can't answer back or tell you about your faults. A cat can't point out your weaknesses. That's why some people would rather love dogs and cats than other people. Yet animals are not of the same essence as humans, and so the love isn't a complete or fulfilling one.

God presented every animal to the man, but none was suitable for him. There was none to whom he could relate, none who could help him in his proprietorship of the earth. So God said, "It's not good for man to be alone in one body." Love cannot dwell alone. It is impossible for love to love alone. So God created the woman, the female-man.

The first principle to note regarding the woman is that she was created as a result of something beautiful. Woman came about because of love; it was love that caused her existence. The primary purpose of the female was to be loved by the male, just as God's major purpose for creating the spirit-man was to give him love. Having dominion was secondary.

What was the method God used to create the female?

The LORD God caused the man to fall into a deep sleep; and while he was sleeping, he took one of the man's ribs and closed up the place with flesh. Then the LORD God made a woman from the rib he had taken out of the man, and he brought her to the man. (Genesis 2:21–22)

God's creation of the female is fascinating because it exactly parallels His creation of man. Just as God had drawn man from Himself and created him as a spiritual being, He drew the woman out of the man and made her a physical being. God, who is love, needed someone to whom to give His love, and so He created man out of Himself. Similarly, the male needed someone to whom to give his love, and so God created the female from the male's own body. This parallel in creation illustrates the oneness and mutual love that God and man and male and female were created to have.

> GOD'S CREATION OF THE FEMALE PARALLELS HIS CREATION OF MAN.

The word "rib" in Genesis 2:22 is the Hebrew word *tsela*. It does not necessarily mean a rib as we understand the word. It could mean "side" or "chamber." In any event, the Scripture is telling us that God drew the woman from a part of the man. Why? It is because the receiver has to be exactly like the giver. Just as man needed to be spirit in order to receive love from God and be in relationship with Him, the woman needed to be of the same essence as man in order to receive love from him and be in relationship with him.

That is why God did not go back to the soil to fashion another house when He formed the female. If He had done that, she would not have been the exact duplicate of the man. She would not have been made of the essence of the male, the way humanity was made of the essence of God. So God took exactly what was needed from the male to make an exact replica, and He created the woman.

Now, while males and females are of the same essence, and while the woman is a replica of the man, God actually made them using different methods. The Bible says that the man was "*formed*" of the dust of the earth. (See Genesis 2:7.) The Hebrew word for formed is *yatsar*, meaning to mold, as a potter molds clay. However, the Bible says that God "*made*" the woman. (See Genesis 2:22.) The Hebrew word for made is *banah*, which means to "build" or "construct."

When Paul said in 1 Corinthians 11:8, "*Man did not come from woman, but woman from man*," he was referring to this passage in Genesis. God took the woman out of the man and built her. This is how I picture it: God built her by multiplying cells that He had taken from the man, similar to what happens in the womb after a fertilized egg is implanted there. The cells begin to multiply, and a new human being begins to be constructed.

So there was this beautiful structuring in the creation of woman. When God had finished making her, she was exactly like the man. She was so much in likeness to him that, when God presented her to the man, his first words were, "*This is now bone of my bones and flesh of my flesh; she shall be called 'woman,' for she was taken out of man*" (Genesis 2:23). The man's words are both beautiful and instructive. Something that is built has the same components as the material from which it is made or from which it comes. Therefore, God built the female out of the part that He took from the male so that they would be made of exactly the same substance.

A PERFECT COMPLEMENT

The female-man is the perfect complement to the male-man. She is man because she came from man and has a spirit. Her physical house is also like the male's. She is bone of his bones and flesh of his flesh. She is the same as a man, and that is why she can give and receive love and be in relationship with him.

A DISTINCT CREATION

Because the female came from the male, the male is essentially the giver, and the female is essentially the receiver. Thus, God fashioned the woman to be the receiver. If you look at the way the female body is made, she is a receiver from A to Z. This is part of the purpose for which she was created. Her receiving complements the male's giving. The woman is like the man because the receiver has to be exactly like the giver. However, in order for the woman to be the receiver, she also has to be different from the man.

Though the woman was taken from the man and was built to be like him, she is a distinct creation. This is highlighted in her physical difference from the man in that she is able to bear children. You could say that

> THE FEMALE IS BOTH THE SAME AS AND DIFFERENT FROM THE MALE.

a woman is a "wombed man." She is a man with a womb. She is still the same as a male, but she has certain differences. These differences are complementary in nature and are designed so that the male and female can fulfill one another's emotional and physical needs while they are spiritually nourished by God and His love, and so that together they can fulfill their mandate to have dominion over the world.

DIFFERENT BY DESIGN

Males and females were created both similarly and differently in order to fulfill God's purposes. Remember the two main principles of purpose?

+ The purpose of something determines its nature (or design).
+ The nature of something determines its needs.

Men and women were created with complementary designs that reflect their individual roles in the larger purposes for which they were created. In the next chapter we'll look at the implications of their complementary roles and discover what put their perfect symmetry out of balance.

PRINCIPLES

1. God created man for relation and vocation.

2. Man was created to be loved by God.

3. Man was created as spirit.

4. Man was created to have dominion over the world.

5. Man was placed within two physical houses: the male and the female.

6. The male is essentially a giver, and the female is essentially a receiver.

7. The male was created to give love, and the female was created to receive love.

8. Men and women are of the same essence but have different designs.

9. Men and women have complementary designs in order to fulfill their purposes.

CHAPTER THREE STUDY QUESTIONS

QUESTIONS FOR REFLECTION

1. Read Genesis 1:27: "*So God created man in his own image, in the image of God he created him; male and female he created them.*" What does it mean to be created in the image of God? Does your understanding of your creation in God's image have an effect on your relationship with God and how you live your life?

EXPLORING GOD'S PRINCIPLES AND PURPOSES

2. When God created humanity, what two overarching purposes did He have in mind? (p. 57)

    _____ and _____

3. Why does God desire to share His love with us? (p. 58)

4. You cannot love without doing what? (p. 59) _____

5. In the Garden of Eden, when humanity rejected God's ways, why didn't God start over and make a new race of men? (p. 59)

6. God created mankind as spirit, and spirits have no _____. (p. 60)

7. God used two physical forms to express the one entity of man in order to fulfill His _____ _____. (p. 61)

8. The essence of both male and female is the resident spirit within them, called "_____." (p. 61)

9. Men and women often end up battling one another for supremacy, as if one needs to prove superiority over the other. Why is neither superior to the other? (p. 63)

10. Genesis 1:26–27 indicates that the process through which God created man was different from the process through which God formed the male and female. We can think of the distinction in this way: God _____ man, but He _____ male and female. (p. 65)

11. The first principle to note regarding the woman is that she was created as a result of something _____. It was _____ that caused her existence. (p. 67)

12. What did the man say when God presented the woman to him? (p. 68)

13. Because the female came from the male, the male is essentially the _____, and the female is essentially the _____. (p. 69)

14. Why were the male and female designed with complementary differences? (p. 69)

CONCLUSION

God created humanity for a relationship of love with Himself and for the vocation of exercising dominion over the earth and reflecting God's nature and purposes in the spiritual realm. Male and female were created so mankind could fulfill its dominion responsibilities in a physical world while experiencing the blessings of human oneness and love. Males and females were designed both similarly and differently in order to fulfill God's plans. Their complementary differences reflect their individual roles in the eternal purposes for which they were created.

APPLYING GOD'S PRINCIPLES TO YOUR LIFE

THINKING IT OVER

+ Are the two overarching purposes for which you were created—relationship with God and family and exercising dominion—the central focus of your life? Why or why not?

+ Have you allowed your spiritual life to become dependent on the spiritual life of your spouse, or are you developing a personal relationship with God yourself? Are you waiting for your husband or wife to become a Christian before you will enter fully into the Christian life? Think about the fact that you are an individual spiritual being and are directly responsible to God for your spiritual life. Will you devote yourself to loving God with all your heart, soul, mind, and strength—no matter what others around you may do or say?

PRAYING ABOUT IT

+ Ask God to show you how you can better fulfill your purposes of relation and vocation. Write down what you feel He is saying to you and share it with your spouse, prayer partner, or pastor. Ask for prayer support in these vital areas of your life.

+ Have you seen yourself as a complement to your mate and others of the opposite gender, or do you feel you are working at cross-purposes? Ask God to help you see your differences as complementary and to use them for your mutual benefit and His glory.

ACTING ON GOD'S TRUTH

+ Commit to memory the two Scripture passages that emphasize mankind's dominion role in the earthly and spiritual realms: Genesis 1:26–28 and Ephesians 3:10–11. Meditate on these verses daily until they have renewed your mind regarding your God-given purpose.

Through both the spiritual and physical realms, it has been given to man to reflect the love, wisdom, creativity, power, and glory of God.

FOUR

GOD'S DESIGN: EQUAL AND DIFFERENT

He created them male and female and blessed them.
And when they were created, he called them "man."
—Genesis 5:2

Men and women are equal. What we've learned about the purpose and creation of humanity in the last chapter is the basis for their equality:

+ Man was created in the image of God.

+ Man has a spirit.

+ Male and female are both man.

+ The spirit-man resides within both male and female.

+ Both male and female have direct spiritual access to God and are responsible to Him.

+ Both male and female were given dominion over the earth.

Regardless of what culture and society may say, the highest worth and dignity were given to the female by God in creation. She was created equal with the man and was given the task, along with the male, of having dominion over the earth and fulfilling God's purposes in both the physical and spiritual realms.

PURPOSE, NATURE, AND DESIGN

Purpose determines design, and design determines needs. God created man and placed the man in the male and the female. The male was created for a specific purpose, and the female was created for a specific purpose. The purposes of each are related to their overall purpose—to have a relationship of love with God and to have dominion over the earth.

Again, it is the manufacturer who determines the design of a product, and it is the manufacturer who establishes the differences in his products.

Therefore, God designed the male and the female in the forms He determined would best fulfill their purposes.

Males and females are not ultimately different in nature because society has imposed its standards on them; they are not different because of environment; they are not different because of family upbringing or culture. Men's opinions throughout history did not make males and females different. Males and females are different because of their design in creation.

> MALES AND FEMALES ARE DIFFERENT BECAUSE OF THEIR PURPOSE AND DESIGN.

What society and culture have done is to take the intrinsic differences between males and females, distort them, and use them to devalue women. Over the years, it's been proven that our cultural hang-ups about women were wrong. Women have been treated terribly throughout history. Recently, however, when they started to take on new roles, many men discovered—to their amazement—that women are valuable and significant contributors in the world. However, this was God's purpose even before the male and female were made. God made the woman with worth, dignity, purpose, and skill. He planned her design from the beginning.

GOD'S PURPOSE STANDS

If you try to change the design of something, you're looking for trouble. For example, everything that is in your car was put there by the manufacturer, and he knows why he put it there. You can decide, "I want the battery in the trunk." You have the authority to move the battery, because it is your car. You can take the battery out of the engine and put it in the trunk. However, then try to start your car. It won't work. Over the years, we've been trying to change the design of people, and that won't work, either. We need to understand God's purpose.

When Jesus first began to speak with the Samaritan woman at the well, she was wary of Him. She spoke to Him only in the context of the prejudices between the Samaritans and the Jews that prevailed at that time. *"You are a Jew and I am a Samaritan woman. How can you ask me for a drink?"* (John 4:9). He answered her, "If you only knew who you were speaking with." The woman had a problem, and it was not that she was being rude. She thought that since Jesus was a Jew and she was a Samaritan woman, He wouldn't speak with her. She didn't know who He really was. He said, "If you only knew who was talking to you, everything would be all right. However, I know you don't know, so go ahead and talk foolishly for a few minutes." He allowed her to be foolish. Then He said, "Let Me tell you who I am," and He began to reveal to her the deep secrets of her heart. After that, she changed the way she thought about Him. She said, "You're not just a Jew; You're a prophet." She went into the town and said, *"Come, see a man who told me everything I ever did"* (John 4:29). She didn't say, "Come, see a Jew" but *"Come, see a man."* (See John 4:5–30.) People will change their perspective toward you when they know why you're here, when they begin to understand your purpose.

I believe that half of the things we hate about others are qualities that can actually benefit us. However, we usually hate what we don't understand. Over the last twenty-three years that I have been walking with the Lord, I have concluded that when a person doesn't like someone else, the person needs grace because he lacks understanding. He or she is merely in a present state of ignorance. People have hatred, bitterness, and envy toward one another because they are ignorant of God's purposes. This is what has happened between men and women.

When I was in college, I read various psychologists' theories on human nature. Each one seemed to believe that he had a handle on the nature of mankind. Yet their books are now becoming obsolete because psychology has made new discoveries that these psychologists didn't know about when they wrote their books. No one knows the product like the one who made it. God says, *"My purpose will stand"* (Isaiah 46:10). We're just starting to catch up with what God already knows about human nature—because He designed it.

Everything is the way it is because of its purpose. The purpose is what we need to discover, because it explains the design.

THE DOMINION MANDATE

Males and females were designed to exercise dominion over the earth. In the last chapter, we learned that God *"created them male and female and blessed them. And when they were created, he called them 'man'"* (Genesis

5:2). When God created the male and the female, He told them, in effect, "You are manifested in two different bodies, with two different natures, but both male and female—together—are man." He also blessed them, affirming them in their similarities and differences. Therefore, "man" is the spirit that lives inside both male and female. It is this spirit that relates to God and has dominion over the earth.

> THEIR BASIC ASSIGNMENT IS THE SAME, BUT THE EXECUTION OF IT IS DIFFERENT.

God made the products to fulfill their purpose. The female and the male both have dominion, yet they each execute this overall purpose in a different manner. Their basic assignment is the same, but the execution of it is different. Because men and women have different specific purposes, different designs, and different physical bodies, their authority is manifested and carried out in different ways. In the chapters that follow, we will explore the uniqueness of the woman as well as the specific purposes of females and males that enable them to fulfill their dominion assignment.

Again, the basis of the equality of men and women is the fact that they were both created in God's image and that man, the spirit, lives within both male and female. The differences are only functional. That is, the different ways in which the assignment is carried out does not affect their equality; it only reflects their different purposes, designs, and needs.

I am convinced that there can be no dominion unless this original design is intact. It is crucial for us to understand the principle that the way you are is because of why you are. The way a male is and the way a female is are directly related to why they exist. They are different because of what they are called to do.

Therefore, when we look at this beautiful, fascinating, and complex creature called man, who is manifested as both male and female, we must understand that the purposes of men and women determine their individual natures, designs, and needs. This fact explains why the two are so similar and yet so different. Let us now look at these differences more closely to see their implications.

EQUAL AND DIFFERENT

We must continually keep in mind that God created men and women *equal*—and He created them *different*. When Adam first saw the woman, he said something that women have forgotten—and men don't want to remember. God made the woman from the man's rib, or side, and then He presented her to the man. When Adam saw the woman, I believe that he struck the most powerful blow for equality when he said, "*This is now bone of my bones*" (Genesis 2:23). In other words, he was saying, "This person is exactly like me in structure." Second, he said, "'*This is now…flesh of my flesh*' (v. 23). She is exactly like me in all of her physical qualities and in all of her emotional and psychological ability." Yet Adam saw two differences. "We are the same; we are equal," he said, "but there are differences. You have a womb, and you are a receiver."

> ADAM SAID SOMETHING WOMEN HAVE FORGOTTEN AND MEN DON'T WANT TO REMEMBER.

The major difference between a man and a woman is that the woman has a womb and can bear children. Again, you could say that the woman is a "wombed-man." The womb gives the woman a different component in the human makeup. Therefore, God put different "circuits" into the wombed-man in order to operate this component. The woman is the same as the man; she's just like the man. However, her womb requires that her circuits function a little differently in order to allow the womb to fulfill its purpose.

Another difference between a man and a woman is that the woman is designed primarily as a receiver, and the man is designed primarily as a giver. This, of course, does not imply that a woman does not give. On the contrary, her nature is to give and keep on giving. What this means is that the woman was taken out of the man at creation, and that she was designed to receive his love. It means that she was made to be a receiver. In this role, she has many qualities that complement the man, which we call differences.

DIFFERENT DOES NOT MEAN INFERIOR OR SUPERIOR

Even though we all know that differences between men and women exist, most of us have problems with this fact because we believe that being "different" means being inferior or superior to others—especially inferior. Don't confuse being different with being lesser. Different does not imply inferiority or superiority; different simply means different. A woman is not less than a man because she is a woman, and a man is not more than a woman because he's a man. They are both man, but they are different. Their differences are necessary because of their purposes. We need to teach this truth to our children when they are young. We need to say, "Son, your sister is different, not because she's less or because she's more; she's different because of her purpose, and so are you." Some woman say, "I am superior to a man because I have the ability to bear children." Yet it takes two to conceive a child. Everyone has a role. Everyone is equal, but different.

All of us have a fingerprint that no one before us ever had and no one after us will ever have. This distinction is an indication of how God created all of us to be different—and how He wants us to remain distinct, even in our unity with others. It's sad when a person tries to become like somebody else. If you try to be like somebody else, you are preventing yourself from being who you were created to be. You shouldn't try to be like anyone else, because if you try to be like somebody else, you are missing God's best for you.

GOD MADE YOU FOR A SPECIAL PURPOSE. On television, I saw a picture of a little child, with a caption that said, "missing." The Lord spoke to me and said, "I have many children who are missing." Some of you may be missing. You are present in the world, but missing in regard to fulfilling the specific purposes for which you were created. You are behaving like someone else instead of yourself. God is saying to you, "I want you to stop trying to be like someone else and be who you are." God has special plans for you, if you will be who He created you to be. He has given you your personality and gifts for a specific reason. *"For we are God's workmanship, created in Christ Jesus to do good works, which God prepared in advance for us to do"* (Ephesians 2:10). Paul said, *"Follow my example, as I follow the example of Christ"* (1 Corinthians 11:1). In other words, he was saying, "When I look like Christ, imitate me." The only thing we are to imitate in people is the life of Christ. Otherwise, we're not to try to imitate others.

God made you different because of the purpose He had in mind for you. The same thing is true for everyone else. We run into trouble when we try change people into what we are. This often happens when people get married. After the honeymoon, people start to try to make their spouses think and behave as they do. The greatest problem in marriage is when one party tries to make the other party over. That person is already made. People spend years trying to change their mates. But God made males and females different because of what they were designed to do. That means your wife is the way she is because of why she is. Your husband is the way he is because of why he is. If you try to make a female a male, or try to make a male a female, you're trying to do the impossible. No one can alter God's purposes. We can try to change God's purposes, but they will always remain the same. Remember that God has said, "Before My purpose could be changed, I would have to stop being God."

If you are going to deal with a female, you must find out what God wanted when He made females; otherwise, you're going to be handling something you don't understand. The same thing applies for the male. Thus, everything is the way it is because of its purpose. We need to see our differences as complementary; we need to celebrate our uniqueness as females and males, as well as the individuality God has placed within each person.

THE FALL OF MAN

Men and women were created, therefore, with perfectly complementary designs. When did we start departing from God's original purpose?

The third chapter of Genesis explains the source of the conflict and strife between men and women. In chapter two, we read that God instructed the man, Adam, that he could eat from any tree in the Garden except the Tree of Knowledge of Good and Evil; if he did, he would die. (See Genesis 2:17.) When Eve was created, Adam passed this instruction along to her. The events that followed turned men and women away from God's perfect design. The devil, in the form of a serpent, tempted Eve to eat from the tree, saying that if she did, she would not die but would *be like God, knowing good and evil*" (Genesis 3:5). Eve succumbed to the temptation, Adam agreed, and they both ate of the fruit of the tree.

MEN AND WOMEN LOST
THEIR PERFECTLY
BALANCED RELATIONSHIP.

By an act of their wills, Adam and Eve rejected God's plans and pursued their own desires. They had been designed to live in God's purposes and under His loving rule. Yet they wanted a purpose for which they were not created. They thought that they could be like God Himself. They weren't satisfied with their position and roles. Yet their rejection of God's purposes only brought them heartache, because they were not meant to live independently from God and the purposes for which He had created them. This Scripture describes their predicament: *"Although they claimed to be wise, they became fools"* (Romans 1:22).

RESULTS OF THE FALL

The first result of the Fall was that humanity's fellowship with God was broken. Remember that man was created to receive God's love. Yet Adam and Eve's sin and rebellion separated them from God. God still loved them, but they no longer had the same open channel to God with which to receive His love.

Second, Adam and Eve experienced death, just as God had said they would. They did not immediately experience physical death; yet the remarkable spirit that God had placed within them, the spirit that distinguished them as made in His image, suffered a death. While they still retained elements of their creation in God's image, they no longer perfectly reflected the nature and character of their Creator. They also were destined to die physically at some point.

Third, Adam and Eve suffered the loss of their perfectly balanced relationship.

To the woman [God] said, "I will greatly increase your pains in child-bearing; with pain you will give birth to children. Your desire will be for your husband, and he will rule over you." To Adam he said, "Because you listened to your wife and ate from the tree about which I commanded you, 'You must not eat of it,' cursed is the ground because of you; through painful toil you will eat of it all the days of your life. It will produce thorns and thistles for you, and you will eat the plants of the field. By the sweat of your brow you will eat your food until you return to the ground, since from it you were taken; for dust you are and to dust you will return." (Genesis 3:16–19)

WAS THE WOMAN CURSED?

We have learned that when purpose is unknown or is rejected, abuse is inevitable. The devaluing of women by men is not a natural consequence of God's original design. Some people claim that this is so, and they use it as a justification for putting women down. Rather, it came about as a result of humanity's rebellion against God and rejection of His purposes. Man and woman cannot function in true harmony and effectiveness outside of God's purposes.

After Adam and Eve rebelled, God made some specific statements to the woman. I want to strongly emphasize that these statements were not curses. I was brought up to believe that God cursed Eve. The teachings of my Sunday school classes insinuated that this is what God did. However, this was not the case. God was telling Eve the natural consequences of rejecting His purposes.

The Bible does not say that God cursed the man or the woman. God said, *"Cursed is the ground"* (Genesis 3:17). In other words, He said to Adam, "It is the earth that is really going to feel the impact of your disobedience. Because of this, you will have to struggle to survive in it." Moreover, He did not curse the woman by making her a child-bearer. He didn't say, "Just for that, now you're going to have children, and it's going to hurt." Adam and Eve were always meant to have children. Eve already had the ability to bear children so that humanity could reproduce after its kind. That ability was established before sin came into the picture. So bearing children is not a curse. Rather, when you bear a child, you are fulfilling part of God's purpose for humanity. However, God told Eve that, because of sin, she was now going to experience pain in childbearing. If there hadn't been a Fall, a woman could have had as many children as she wanted without any pain. God made it clear that pain—not the ability to have the child—was the product of the Fall.

Many women today consider childbearing and child-rearing to be a burden because they do not receive enough support in this from their husbands. Moreover, when a woman is a single parent, the burden becomes even greater. The Scripture says in Genesis 1:28, "*God blessed* **them** *and said to* **them**, *'Be fruitful'*" (emphasis added). Both female and male were supposed to be fruitful. That meant that any babies Eve would bear would belong to both of them. God said to them, in effect, "Don't just concern yourselves with having dominion over the earth together; you have to bring up the children together, too." Part of the result of the Fall may be that too much of this responsibility has fallen to the woman, while the man has been preoccupied with "taking dominion." Sometimes women, also, can be more concerned with involvement in the world than raising their children.

DOMINATION AND DESIRE INSTEAD OF DOMINION

God not only told the woman that her pain in childbearing would be increased, but He also said, "*Your desire will be for your husband, and he will rule over you*" (Genesis 3:16). This is a change from their former relationship. This statement emphasizes the fact that the male and female were originally created to rule together. They were designed to function together equally. God had said to them, "*Fill the earth and subdue it*" (Genesis 1:28). Both of them were supposed to be rulers—and that is still His plan.

After the Fall, both the man and the woman would still rule, but their relationship would become distorted. First, God said to Eve that, because of sin, "*Your desire shall be for your husband*" (v. 16). Once a woman gets married, she has a desire, a longing, for her husband. Sometimes this desire can become controlling. Most of the time this desire is hidden, but it's there. God also told Eve that the man would develop an attitude of rulership over her. He would feel as if he had to dominate her. This was not part of God's plan; however, because of sin, the man's twisted perception of life would cause him to want to dominate the woman, and because of sin, the woman would continually desire to do anything to keep him.

> WOMEN HAVE A TREMENDOUS ABILITY TO ALLOW THINGS.

Most women would not like to admit that they have this desire. However, many marriage counselors can confirm that it exists. They have counseled women who are being abused by men, and they have wondered how these women take it. For example, a man comes home in the middle of the night and beats his wife half dead. He wets the bedclothes because he's been drinking and can't control his bladder. He goes out for three nights in a row, high as a kite, and then comes back home and demands to be fed. His wife allows him to treat her in this manner. She cooks his meals, washes his clothes, and has the bedspread cleaned. Why does she do this? It is this desire.

Women have a tremendous ability to allow things. This isn't entirely a result of the Fall; rather, it is actually a reflection of their creation in God's image. The Bible says that God is long-suffering. This means that He allows things for a long time; He is patient with people, waiting for them to change their behavior. He permits things to go on for a long time. But He's only *long*-suffering; He is not *forever*-suffering. There comes a time when God stops and says, "That's it," and that's when judgment comes. Now, some women get to a point where the desire wears a bit thin. There comes a time when a woman also says, "That's it, brother. After five years of this foolishness, that's it. Get your act together, or judgment is coming down Tuesday morning at 9:00 a.m."

While many women have a limit to their tolerance of abusive behavior, a woman's *tendency* is still this longing for her husband, this desire to please him at all costs. At the same time, the man tends to feel as if he has the right to lord it over her. *"He will rule over you"* (Genesis 3:16). Again, this was not God's plan in creation. God never said that the man in the male was to dominate the man in the female. He said that man—as male and female—was to dominate the earth. The Fall, however, caused the man to have a misplaced and distorted understanding of dominion, so that now the man wants to dominate the woman.

HUMANITY'S REDEEMER

Is humanity doomed to live in the effects of the Fall? Has God's purpose been lost forever? No. His purpose has never changed. His original design still stands. At the very hour of humanity's rejection of God's purpose, God promised a Redeemer who would save men and women from their fallen state and all its ramifications (Genesis 3:15). The Redeemer

> IS GOD'S PURPOSE FOR WOMEN AND MEN LOST FOREVER?

would restore the relationship and partnership of males and females. Jesus Christ is that Redeemer, and because of Him, men and women can return to God's original design for them. Purpose, peace, and potential can return to humanity.

The last two chapters have been an overview of God's purpose for women and men in creation and what happened to derail that purpose. The chapters that follow will help women (and men) apply these purposes in practical ways. They will present the woman's purposes and design and how she relates to the male and his purposes and design.

A return to God's plan, however, means a return to God Himself. It means coming back to God through the Redeemer, yielding your life to Him, and asking Him to fill you with His Holy Spirit so that you will be able to live in His original plan for you. When you do this, God will do an amazing thing. He will cause the human spirit within you, which is dead as a result of the Fall—to come alive again, so that you will be able to reflect His character and His ways. As you return to God and continually yield your spirit to God's Spirit, you will be able to fulfill the purposes for which you were created.

PRINCIPLES

1. Women and men were created equal and different.

2. Everything was designed by God to fulfill its purpose.

3. Females and males are different because of their design.

4. Different does not mean inferior or superior.

5. The purposes of women and men determine their individual nature and needs.

6. The female and male were both given dominion over the earth, yet they each execute this purpose according to their unique purposes and designs.

7. To try to be someone other than what you were created to be is to miss God's best for you.

8. When we try to change God's purposes for ourselves or others, we are attempting the impossible, for God's purposes cannot be altered.

9. Adam and Eve rejected God's purposes by an act of their wills.

10. Because of the Fall, man experienced broken fellowship with God, spiritual and physical death, and the loss of the perfectly balanced relationship between males and females.

11. God did not curse the female or the male as a result of the Fall; He cursed the earth. Adam and Eve experienced the natural consequences of rejecting God and His purposes.

12. Child-bearing is not a curse.

13. As a result of the Fall, the woman has a desire to please her husband and the man has a desire to dominate her.

14. Jesus Christ, the Redeemer, saved humanity from its fallen state and restored the relationship and partnership between males and females.

CHAPTER FOUR STUDY QUESTIONS

QUESTIONS FOR REFLECTION

1. In what ways can people or things be equal but different?

EXPLORING GOD'S PRINCIPLES AND PURPOSES

2. Summarize below what we have discovered so far about the scriptural basis for the equality of men and women. (p. 75)

3. The different ways in which dominion authority is meant to be carried out by males and females does not affect their _____; it reflects only their different _____, _____, and _____. (p. 78)

4. What are two principal characteristics of a woman's physical design that make her different from the male? (p. 79)

5. How and why did humanity depart from God's purpose in creation? (pp. 81–82)

6. What were the results of this departure? (pp. 82–83)

7. Is childbearing a curse on women because of Eve's disobedience to God? Why or why not? (p. 83)

8. Why do many women today consider childbearing and child-rearing to be a burden? (pp. 83–84)

9. In what ways did the perfectly balanced relationship between men and women become distorted after the Fall? (pp. 84–85)

10. Even with the fall of mankind, God's purpose for humanity has _____ _____. (p. 85)

11. How did God intend to restore His relationship with mankind as well as the harmony and balance between men and women so that His eternal purposes could be fulfilled? (pp. 85–86)

CONCLUSION

While men and women were created equal before God, the purposes of males and females determine their different designs, functions, and needs. They are to execute dominion over the earth according to their unique purposes. When men and women are living in harmony, as God intended, their purposes and designs are wonderfully complementary. However, harmony was lost when mankind rebelled against God. Only through redemption in Jesus Christ can men and women be reconciled to God and their harmony with one another be restored so they can fulfill the purposes for which they were created.

APPLYING GOD'S PRINCIPLES TO YOUR LIFE

THINKING IT OVER

+ Have you acknowledged that members of the opposite sex have legitimate differences from you, or do you tend to think less of their design, abilities, and tendencies?

+ Have you accepted your own gender and its differences from the opposite sex? If not, why?

PRAYING ABOUT IT

+ God has special plans for you. He has given you your gender, personality, and gifts for specific and good reasons. Read Jeremiah 1:5. Then ask God to enable you to accept who He created you to be, thanking Him for fulfilling His purposes in your life as you yield yourself to Him and His ways.

Returning to God's original purpose means first returning to God Himself. It means being reconciled to God through the Redeemer, Jesus Christ; yielding your life to your Creator; and asking Him to fill you with His Holy Spirit. Your human spirit—which is dead because of the Fall—will then become alive so that you can reflect God's character and ways. If you have never asked God for forgiveness through Christ and received His Spirit, why don't you do so right now and start living in God's eternal purposes? You can pray a prayer such as this one:

> Heavenly Father,
>
> I want to fulfill the purpose for which I was created. I know that this purpose became distorted through the fall of mankind and my own disobedience to You. However, I want to love and serve You. I come to You now through Your Son Jesus Christ. I ask You to forgive me based on the forgiveness and redemption Jesus provided when He died for my sins on the cross and rose from the dead. Fill me with Your Holy Spirit so that I can truly reflect Your image and likeness. Help me to fulfill the purposes for which You made me. I pray this in the name of Jesus, my Redeemer. Amen.

ACTING ON GOD'S TRUTH

+ If you are trying to change someone, you are attempting the impossible, for (1) you cannot change God's purposes for males and females and individuals, and (2) only He can change a person to become who He created that person to be. Instead of trying to change the other person, pray for him or her daily. Ask God to enable that person to fulfill all the purposes and potential he or she has received through both creation and redemption. Then write down three positive things about the person (gifts, talents, outlook, fruits of the Spirit) and thank God for him or her.

To try to be someone other than you were created to be is to miss God's best for you.

FIVE

THE UNIQUENESS OF WOMAN

*The sun has one kind of splendor, the moon another and the stars
another; and star differs from star in splendor.*
—1 Corinthians 15:41

God did not create the woman as an afterthought, but as an integral part of His plan in creation. As such, He designed and built her in love and with particular care. Her uniqueness is a reflection of God's purposes and design for her.

The principles in this chapter are not a complete list of the woman's uniqueness. Other chapters will cover additional aspects of her distinct nature, such as her primary communication style and emotional needs. However, the following principles highlight important truths about the woman's nature that are essential for us to understand as we learn to know, value, and encourage the woman in what she was created to be.

The female is unique in five significant ways.

THE WOMAN IS GOD'S IDEA

First, a woman is unique because she is God's idea.

Women, you don't understand how special you are. Adam hadn't even imagined the woman, but God had her particularly in mind. In Genesis 2:18, God said, "*It is not good for the man to be alone. I will make a helper suitable for him.*" Adam was fumbling around in the bush thinking up animals' names. God said, "This is not good. This man needs help." So it was God who said that the man needed the woman. She was God's idea.

A woman is a product of God; this makes her God's property. If you handle her, you are handling God's idea. If you curse at a woman, you are cursing at God's idea. If you slap a woman, you are slapping God's idea in the face. If you abandon a woman, you are abandoning God's idea.

Women, no matter what men might say about you, no matter what you might think about yourself, you are a good idea. God's mind thought of you, and God's Spirit brought you into being. You are the result of God's idea, and that makes you very valuable to Him.

THE WOMAN HAS A SPIRIT INSIDE

Second, a woman is unique because she has a spirit inside. This makes her a free and responsible spiritual being.

> A WOMAN HAS HER OWN SPIRIT-BEING WITH WHICH TO WORSHIP GOD.

You can't imagine the power that you will have when you understand the spirit that is inside of you. Spiritually, men and women are equal; they have the same spirit-man within. God called both male and female "man." I like the way the Word of God expresses it: *"There is neither...slave nor free, male nor female"* in the body of Christ (Galatians 3:28). God doesn't look down from heaven today and say, "There are many women and men down there." He says, "There is a lot of man down there."

First Peter 3:4 says that a woman's beauty *"should be that of [her] inner self, the unfading beauty of a gentle and quiet spirit, which is of great worth in God's sight."* It is this *"inner self"* that is a woman's spirit. What the woman is physically is different from what she is in her inner self. The spirit-man inside every woman is the being that relates to God. The next time you women run into somebody who is confused about this concept, just tell them, "Look, I have a female body, but I have a spirit-man inside. I'm female because of what I have to do physically and in God's kingdom on the planet; however, I deal directly with God as a spirit."

Jesus said, *"God is spirit, and his worshipers must worship in spirit and in truth"* (John 4:24). A woman has her own spirit-being with which to worship God. She can bless the Lord and love the Lord and receive from the Lord herself. A woman can preach, not because she's female, but because she has a spirit-man within her.

Because a spirit-man lives within the woman, the treatment of the woman by the man has to be taken very seriously. God honors and respects the woman. He loves and identifies with the spirit-man inside the female, and so He takes special care in regard to her. When you have offended the spirit-man, you have offended God. You have to be careful what you do to the spirit within either the male or the female.

Some men forget that there is a spirit-man inside the woman. If a man impatiently tells a female, "I don't like your moods," he should check to whom he is speaking. There is a spirit inside that precious body. One reason why the Bible tells us not to go to sleep without resolving our anger (see Ephesians 4:26) is that it's very important to treat well those who have been created in the image of God. James reinforced this theme: *"With the tongue we praise our Lord and Father, and with it we curse men, who have been made in God's likeness"* (James 3:9). You see, anger or resentment is a spiritual matter. It's not a physical concern; it's a spiritual one.

Thus, when a man walks around with anger at his wife because she didn't do something he wanted her to do, he should pray! Why? He's dealing with a spirit. Some men say, "I could never forgive my wife." Yet the Spirit of God within us can do anything. The ego might have a problem with it, but the spirit can forgive.

A husband should deal with his wife very delicately, for if he doesn't, God says that his prayers won't be answered. This is not a light matter. The Bible says that men are to treat women with sensitivity and consideration. If they don't, their prayers could be hindered.

> *Husbands, in the same way be considerate as you live with your wives, and treat them with respect as the weaker* [delicate] *partner and as heirs with you of the gracious gift of life, so that nothing will hinder your prayers.* (1 Peter 3:7)

God is saying to men, "Wait a minute. The woman isn't just a body of flesh. She has a spirit. The way you treat her will affect your prayer life." Therefore, if you don't treat a woman with consideration and respect, it could block your relationship with God. God won't hear your prayers until you go back and make things right with her, because you have interfered with the spirit-man in the woman.

> SOME MEN THINK THEY CAN SLAP THEIR WIVES AROUND AND THEN GO TO CHURCH AS IF NOTHING HAD HAPPENED.

Some men think they can slap their wives around and then go to church as if nothing had happened. God isn't buying it. Some men think they can do something to hurt their wives and then go ahead and become a deacon. God isn't listening to their prayers. Mistreating a woman is a serious thing because God deals with the woman's spirit in spirit and in truth. He has so much respect for her spirit that He defends her when she is misused.

Jesus said that if you go to worship God and, while you are offering your gift, you remember that there is a broken relationship in your life that needs to be mended, you must leave your offering right there at the altar and go and make things right. Then you can come back and offer your gift. You shouldn't try to offer it beforehand, because God won't accept it. (See Matthew 5:22–24.) Jesus also talked about the importance of forgiveness in our relationships. He said that if you do not forgive someone who has something against you, or whom you have something against, then the Father will not forgive you and will not hear you. (See Matthew 6:14–15.)

Jesus was saying that relationships with other people are even more important than worship, because you cannot worship except in the context of your relationships. It doesn't matter how serious and sincere you are about God. It doesn't matter how much of the Holy Spirit you possess or how much Scripture you've learned. It doesn't matter to God how many times you speak in tongues or whether you have memorized a tremendous amount of Scripture. God is

> GOD'S ACCEPTANCE OF EVEN YOUR TITHES IS CONTINGENT UPON YOUR RELATIONSHIPS WITH OTHER PEOPLE.

not overly impressed by your ability to communicate with Him, by your ability to articulate your worship, prayer, or praise. His reception of your worship—whether it is through your giving, your praise, your administration of the kingdom of God, or your ministry of the gifts of the Spirit—is contingent upon your relationships with others, especially your spouse. So if you want to give God a thousand dollars, whether or not God receives it depends on whether or not you are in right relationship with others. God's acceptance of even your tithes is contingent upon your relationships with other people, not on how much you give Him.

This truth brings the matter of right relationships between men and women down to where it hurts, doesn't it? We need to clearly understand what God's Word says about the value of women, as well as His purpose for men and women, so that we have no excuse for not mending our broken relationships.

Can you imagine husbands stopping in the middle of Sunday morning worship and stepping outside with their wives to make things right with them? If that were to happen, we'd have a brand new society. Yet I find that people often try the easy route when they have been in conflict with others. They go to God and say, "God, please forgive Mary." Or they say, "God, tell Mary that I forgive her," or, "God, I ask You to change Mary." They don't want to go to the person directly. We love to hide behind God so that we don't have to accept the responsibility of face-to-face relationships. Our reluctance to deal honestly and directly with other people is the reason why there are so many problems in relationships, even in the body of Christ. We use God as a scapegoat.

I honor my wife and do right by her, not only because I love her and because of who she is, but also for the sake of my relationship with God. Jesus said that my relationship with God is even more important than my relationship with my wife—and yet God made my relationship with Him contingent on my relationship with her.

THE WOMAN WAS TAKEN OUT OF MAN

Third, the woman is unique because she was taken out of man.

THE WOMAN'S ORIGIN

First Corinthians 11:8 says, *"Man did not come from woman, but woman from man."* According to our Manufacturer, man was taken out of the soil, but woman was taken out of man. The implications of this are striking and significant. Something that has been taken from something else has the same components as that from which it was derived. Adam wasn't ignorant of who the woman was. He said, *"This is now bone of my bones and flesh of my flesh"* (Genesis 2:23). She was part of him; she was like him. He said, *"She shall be called 'woman'"* (v. 23). Why? *"For she was taken out of man"* (v. 23).

The female is what she is because she came out of what the male is. Remember that man is spirit because man came out of God, who is Spirit.

Therefore, humanity must stay connected to God in order to have spiritual life. In the same way, since woman came out of man, she needs to stay connected to man in order to live the life she was created to live. Any woman who decides that she is an island unto herself is going to become a volcano before too long.

A man really can't get upset about what a woman is. He can't forget the material of which she is made—the same material of which he is made. Because of this, she should be valued and loved by the man.

> *Husbands ought to love their wives as their own bodies. He who loves his wife loves himself. After all, no one ever hated his own body, but he feeds and cares for it, just as Christ does the church—for we are members of his body.* (Ephesians 5:28–30)

Paul said that if you take proper care of your body, it shows that you love yourself. A husband is to love his wife as he loves himself, as his own body. However, too often we fail to apply this principle in marriage, and in the general relationships of men and woman. Males and females are of the same essence and therefore should respect and love one another. Jesus reinforced this principle when He said that one of the greatest commandments is, *"Love your neighbor as yourself"* (Matthew 19:19). If we really understood this truth, there would be more patience, understanding, and forgiveness among men and women.

THE WOMAN'S POSITION

"Man did not come from woman, but woman from man" (1 Corinthians 11:8). The entire eleventh chapter of 1 Corinthians is talking about the position of men and women and about the male-female relationship. It's talking about authority.

Some people feel that Paul was being a chauvinist when he made the above statement. Rather, he was referring to the creation of male and female. He made an important distinction between the spiritual position of men and women and the male-female relationship. In doing so, he used a spiritual example because he did not want his statements to be misinterpreted.

SOME PEOPLE FEEL THAT PAUL WAS A CHAUVINIST.

Paul was saying, in effect, "Look, some of you women think that I am trying to put you down or say that you are inferior. Therefore, in order to make myself clear, let me explain to both men and women the true nature of authority." In verse three, he said, *"Now I want you to realize that the head of every man is Christ."* So first we see that the man has a head to whom he is responsible. He is under the headship of Christ. Verse three continues, *"And the head of the woman is man."* The woman also has a head. She is responsible to the man. The verse concludes, *"And the head of Christ is God."* Paul was expressing this idea: "If you think you don't like being under somebody else's authority, you will have to tell Jesus to move out from under the Father's authority. Until you become better than Jesus, the best thing to do is to stay under your authority."

A woman may be smarter, have more education, work a more prestigious job, or make more money than a man. Yet for the man to fulfill his role, she needs to submit to him. Submission is an act of the will, a choice. A woman should submit to a man, not because the man says so, and not because society says so, but because of her purpose. In this way, she enables her husband to be a leader.

There is an evil spirit abroad in the world today in which nobody wants to be under anybody else. This satanic spirit has taken over our society. Yet Jesus Himself gave us our model of authority and submission when He submitted to His Father. Philippians 2:6–8 says,

> [Jesus] *being in very nature God, did not consider equality with God something to be grasped, but made himself nothing, taking the very nature of a servant, being made in human likeness. And being found in appearance as a man, he humbled himself and became obedient to death—even death on a cross!*

Even though Jesus is equal to God, He submitted Himself to the Father and to the Father's plan. The prophet Isaiah talked about both the deity and humility of God the Son. He said, in essence, "You aren't going to believe this report. A Son will be born, and His name shall be called Wonderful Counselor, the Mighty God." (See Isaiah 9:6.)

We might well ask, "But Isaiah, you just said, *'For unto us a Child is born, unto us a Son is given'* (v. 6 NKJV). What do you mean that this

Child, this Son, will be called Mighty God? How can He be God and Son?"

Isaiah's answer would be, "He is God, but He took on the position of Man and Servant for the sake of your redemption."

Purpose necessitated the position. The purpose of God was redemption. The Godhead said, "Somebody has to go down and submit to us in order to bring about the salvation of man." So the Word of God, who is God Himself, said, "I'll go. I know I am an equal in the Godhead, but for the purpose of redemption, I will be made in the likeness of man and will submit."

Jesus is not inferior to Jehovah; They are equal. But for the purpose of salvation, He submitted Himself to a position in which He could fulfill the requirements of salvation. Similarly, a woman isn't any less than her husband; however, for God's purposes, it is her position to submit.

Do you know why marriages and relationships and society aren't working? It is because people are refusing to accept their positions. What if the tires on your car decided they wanted to take on the role of the steering wheel? The whole car wouldn't be able to move. This is the stalemate that our society is in. Everybody wants the same position. Nobody wants to trust anybody.

Many of you women have had your hearts broken in the past by unsympathetic and domineering men. God has compassion on you. He has made provision for your hurt through the grace and blood of Jesus Christ and the healing power of His Holy Spirit. Yet your hurt can't change God's original design for males and females. He can't alter His design based on your ideas of what a relationship should be, even though you have had painful experiences.

Some of our problems are the result of our own ignorance. The reason things haven't worked out for some of us is that we made the wrong decision in the beginning. Many women have prayed, "Lord, if I had known what I know now, I wouldn't have married this fellow." The Word of God says, "When you got married, you didn't sin. Whatever circumstances you find yourself in, stay there. Submit yourself to the position you're supposed to be in." (See 1 Corinthians 7:17, 28, 36.)

You have to understand your position.

First Corinthians 11:5–6 says,

Every woman who prays or prophesies with her head uncovered dishonors her head—it is just as though her head were shaved. If a woman does not cover her head, she should have her hair cut off; and if it is a disgrace for a woman to have her hair cut or shaved off, she should cover her head.

Paul was using an illustration to explain the concept of position. A woman should have her head covered, just like a man should have his head covered, just like Christ should have His head covered. Head covering doesn't ultimately refer to hats or veils. Wearing a hat is good, but it doesn't make you any more righteous. Paul was talking about the nature of authority. He was saying, "Look, the man is under Jesus, and Jesus is under the Father. The woman is under the man, and the children are under both of them." Woman was taken out of man, which means that man is her covering by virtue of the way she was created. There is no way to change this. No psychologist can change this. Every time we try to change God's purposes, we cause ourselves problems.

> **YOUR POSITION HAS TO DO WITH YOUR PURPOSE AND DESIGN.**

Our positions have nothing to do with how we feel about them; they have to do with our purpose. What is your purpose? That determines where you are placed. *"For man did not come from woman, but woman from man; neither was man created for woman, but woman for man"* (1 Corinthians 11:8–9). God created man and placed him within the male and the female. Then He subjected the male to Christ Jesus, and the female to the male. If we do not understand our positions, we will function in ignorance, and the results will be pain and destruction. People perish because of a lack of knowledge. (See Proverbs 29:18.)

I suggest to you men that you have no right to have your wife submit to you if you yourself don't submit to anybody else. You are exercising illegal authority if you are demanding submission without being submitted. As a matter of fact, you can't really discipline your children if you're not disciplined yourself.

The male-man needs to be under authority before he is able to exercise it properly. It's impossible for you to say you are the head of a home when you aren't submitted to anybody else. The head of Christ is God, and the head of man is Christ, and the head of woman is man. Any man who is out from under Christ is not really a qualified authority. The most dangerous man to marry is a man who isn't submitted to anyone else, who believes he is the ultimate boss and won't answer to anyone. If a man has to answer to someone, then his wife has someone to whom to appeal.

A woman might not be able to get through to her husband. Some of you women are married to such males. They are so stubborn, their heads are as hard as rocks. But if a man is submitted to God, you can deal with him from the top down.

Remember what Esther did? She wanted to effect a change in her country, but she was afraid to go in to her husband, the king. So she went to God, and God gave her wisdom about what to do. He gave her a plan, and the plan worked. (See Esther 1–10.) You can appeal to the one whose authority the man is under. That is why it is good to have a husband who is responsible to spiritual authority, who is responsible to God.

"*A man ought not to cover his head, since he is the image and glory of God; but the woman is the glory of man*" (1 Corinthians 11:7). Paul was saying that once the man is covered with Christ, his marriage is under authority. However, the woman then needs the man to cover her. First Corinthians 11:9–10 says, "*Neither was man created for woman, but woman for man. For this reason, and because of the angels, the woman ought to have a sign of authority on her head.*"

What do angels have to do with this? You could substitute the term "spirit-world" or "spiritual realm" for the word "*angels*." Paul is saying to the female, "When you start functioning in the kingdom of God, you must be careful, because even the angels will look to see if you are under authority before they will submit to your request. Because of the angels, because of the spirits, you must submit to your authority.

SUBMISSION ACTIVATES HEAVEN.

Why? If you don't, the spirits will not submit to you. They won't do what you ask, and you will lose your spiritual authority."

If you are a female, and you want to do a work for God, all of heaven is ready to work for you. God says, "All right, we'll do spiritual work, but how are your relationships in the natural realm?" Any woman who goes on a missionary journey saying, "I don't need the church; I can do this by myself," isn't going to find any angels supporting her. She can pray in tongues, wear a hat, and carry a big Bible. It won't mean anything to the angels. The angels are looking for your authority. They will ask, "Who are you under? How can you tell us what to do when you yourself aren't under anybody?" Submission activates heaven.

Consider the example of Christ again. How did He submit Himself as a man? When He went to John the Baptist to be baptized, John was in charge. Jesus told him, in effect, "John, you have to do this. You're the one on the scene right now. I understand authority, so you need to baptize Me." John said, "You should baptize me!" Jesus answered, "No, because if you don't baptize Me, the angels aren't going to cooperate with Me, and I'm the Son of God. Baptize Me, so that I can fulfill what God has ordained." (See Matthew 3:14–17.)

Now, if Christ submitted because of heaven, who do we think we are? You may be independent, famous, a fantastic businessperson, and doing very well. However, if you aren't going to submit to anyone, I have problems with you, because heaven doesn't trust you. Don't ever believe that you can run off and do God's work without being in submission. Don't ever run away from a ministry and do your own work because somebody there made you upset. The angels are watching. You can actually remove God's protective covering from yourself when you move out from under your authority. This principle applies to both males and females.

Everyone should be connected with a local church or ministry because of the need for submission. I know people who say, "My pastor is a TV preacher." But a person can't have a relationship of spiritual submission with a TV preacher. At five o'clock on a Tuesday afternoon, when you need the pastor, the TV program isn't on. Who is your pastor then? Covering is a key to God's resources. If you're covered, He'll bless you.

THE SOURCE IS RESPONSIBLE FOR THE PRODUCT.

THE WOMAN'S PROVISION

Let's look now at some additional implications of the man's headship over the woman. The statement, *"Man did not come from woman, but woman from man"* (1 Corinthians 11:8), means that the source is responsible for the product. If Ford produces a car, Ford has to take responsibility for the car. Similarly, the man is responsible for the woman, because she came from man. This is God's original plan. Now, if a man starts thinking that this is *his* plan, rather than God's, his responsibility for the woman will turn into domination over the woman. We have to understand that this is God's design, or we will misuse and abuse it.

The man is responsible for providing for the woman because of his position in the relationship of things. The woman is always supposed to be able to go to her source to receive whatever she needs. There is a parallel to this in the spiritual realm. Spiritually, we are to go to God for what we need. Jesus has told us, "I am the Vine; you are the branches, which receive nourishment from the Vine. Remain in Me." (See John 15:4–5.) So it is with the female and the male.

God says that the woman should remain connected to her source. She should be able to go to the man and get answers. If you are a married woman, and you have a question, ask your husband. If he doesn't have the answer, then go to the next man who is in godly authority. This also applies to a woman who is not married. The man could be your father, your pastor, or your big brother in the Lord, as long as it is someone who represents God as source and provider. That person should be able to give you guidance. Of course, a woman's ultimate Source and Provider is God, and she can always turn to Him. But God has designed things so that the female can receive earthly provision through the male.

"Neither was man created for woman, but woman for man" (1 Corinthians 11:9). Have you noticed the mystery in this statement? The man was not made for the woman, but the woman for the man. This means that the woman was made for whatever the man has. All of his money—she was made for it. All of his vision—she was made for it. All of his dreams—she was made to help bring them to pass. All of his hopes—she was made to help see that they become reality. She was made for everything about the man. This means that when a man buys a car, she drives it. When he

receives a bonus, she shares it. It's like when a man takes his wife out for dinner and says, "What do you want? I'll buy you anything on the menu." After they order and their meals come, she looks over at his dinner and says, "Hmmm. That looks really good." So she ends up eating his dinner instead of the one she ordered. Does that sound familiar? Whatever the man has, she was made for it.

My wife was made for everything that I have. Her mental faculties were made for me. Her physical body was made for me. Everything in the female was made for the man, including her intellectual ability. How many men believe this? A woman's mind is an awesome machine. God gave the woman a way of thinking that will amaze you. If you take a little thought, a little idea, and drop it into a woman's mind, you'll never get a simple idea back—you'll get a fully developed plan. Do you know why many men turn the running of the home over to their wives? A woman can take a mortgage that's overdue or a business that's falling apart, and say, "You sit down; let me handle this." She knows how to get you through these things. She can dig you out of a hole. The sad thing is that when some men get out of the hole, they proceed to walk over their wives. The unique qualities and contributions of the woman must be valued by the man.

THE WOMAN'S INTERDEPENDENCE

"In the Lord, however, woman is not independent of man, nor is man independent of woman. For as woman came from man, so also man is born of woman. But everything comes from God" (1 Corinthians 11:11–12). Everything comes full cycle. After all that Paul had said up to this point, he then placed both male and female in the same spiritual position. He said, "In the Lord, both man and woman are the same. Woman came from man, but no man comes into this world unless he is born of a woman. God has ordained both the spiritual and the physical realms, and each has its purpose."

Again, spiritually, women and men are equal. My wife and I are equal before the Lord. She can go before the Lord and get the same spiritual help that I get. She doesn't need to go through her husband. That is why, if you are a single mother, your spirit can go to God and do business with Him. You don't need to get permission from man to go to God; you have a spirit-man within.

The essence of the matter is this: in the spiritual realm, there is no difference between men and women, but in the physical realm, there has to be the proper relationship of submission. I was speaking to a precious lady who has

> **"AT WORK, I'M THE BOSS, BUT AT HOME, I'M A WIFE."**

a management job at an insurance company. She told me, "You know, at work, I'm the boss. Yet when I walk through the door into my home, I'm a wife." That's a smart woman. Of course, you can be the boss at work. But when you get home, you're a wife. That means you can't treat your husband like your employees at the office. An altogether different authority takes over. You can preach all you want, prophecy, rebuke the devil, and cast out twenty thousand demons; however, when you go home, your husband is in authority. Yet he has to understand that he's still supposed to be in the Lord when he's in the home. A woman should not be subjected to pride and foolishness from her husband when she is in the home.

THE WOMAN IS PHYSICALLY DIFFERENT

Fourth, a woman is unique because she is physically different from a man. She is a spirit-man with a female body.

THE WOMAN IS DELICATE

First Peter 3:7 says, "*Husbands, in the same way be considerate as you live with your wives, and treat them with respect as the weaker partner and as heirs with you of the gracious gift of life.*"

The woman is unique because she is a physical being who is "*weaker.*" The word "*weaker*" here isn't referring just to physical strength, because many women are stronger than many men. Women can put up with much adversity and still survive. Many men couldn't handle what women handle. I like to translate the word "*weaker*" as "more delicate." Peter was saying, "Husband, treat your wife with consideration and respect, because God designed her in such a way that she is delicate. She is very, very fine."

Remember that God took a scoop of dirt with which to fashion the male, but He built the woman. God built the female a little more elegantly. Her shape is a little more refined than a man's. He designed her delicately. I believe this also refers to the delicacy of her soul. The expression of a woman's soul is very refined because of her purpose; she is more sensitive.

I believe that the definition of *"weaker"* should go even deeper to indicate that the woman is more "absorbent." She can absorb things more easily than a man, because she was created to absorb. That is why God told the husband to be careful what he stimulated her with, to be careful how he treated her. Why? She is so delicate that she absorbs everything around her.

THE WOMAN IS A "WOMBED-MAN"

Some women want to be the same as a man both spiritually and physically. However, God didn't make the female to be the same as the male. He made her physically different to fulfill a purpose. Purpose determines design, and design determines needs. A man's physical purpose and a woman's physical purpose are different. If men and women don't understand this, and they try to become the same, there are going to be problems.

God designed the female to be physically different from the male so that she could bear the offspring of the race. She is the "wombed-man." She was meant to receive the seed of the man, conceive, and carry the child until it is born. In this way, God entrusted the woman with a major role in the furtherance and survival of the human race. The purpose of something determines its design, and God designed everything to fulfill its purpose. If you know the purpose of something, you can appreciate why the design is different. The female's purpose is distinct from the male's purpose—she is designed to bear children—and therefore God made each of them unique.

THE WOMAN'S NATURE IS INBORN

What has been happening in our society, however, is that people have been trying to change their designs. There are women who want to be like men, and there are men who want to be like women. God is saying to them, "You don't have the circuits for it." To pursue these desires is the equivalent of short-circuiting. People are living static lives in which they don't know their purpose. They can't appreciate why people are different.

Imagine a car battery saying, "I want to be a carburetor," and trying to function as a carburetor. The car won't work. Batteries and carburetors are different because they have different functions. Although their differences make them valuable, a carburetor isn't anything without a battery. No matter how they might feel about one another, they still need each other, because they are both integral parts of something larger—the car. We must understand that males and females are all part of something larger, called man. Yet they are different, because they have different purposes.

If you are not sure that you are a female, God has provided you with physical evidence so that you may know. If you were born with a female reproductive system, you are a female. If you were not, you are a male. How you feel and whom you prefer to sleep with are not relevant. These things don't make you a woman or a man. Your feelings do not bring dignity to that which is unnatural. The fact that many people are doing something does not mean that it is right. We shouldn't confuse numbers with normalcy. If enough of us are abnormal, we'll believe that we are normal. Don't let anybody fool you into believing that you're something that you're not. You should look to your design.

WE SHOULDN'T CONFUSE NUMBERS WITH NORMALCY.

The male is designed to provide seed for the purpose of procreation. Therefore, if you are not sure that you are a female, check to see if you were meant to provide sperm. If you were not, then you are a woman. Whether or not you can provide a climax is not the issue. If you are not a male, you should live as the woman you were designed to be, so that you can fulfill your true purpose.

Forget all the psychological, emotional, and sociological explanations. The only qualification for being a specific gender is to be born with the organs that enable you to fulfill the purpose of that gender. Having an operation and changing your sex organs does not change your nature. If you change your sex organs, it is just like having a kidney transplant. You are still who you were born to be. If a male receives a female's kidney in a kidney transplant, he's still a man.

So spiritually, we deal with the spirit-man within us, but physically, we deal with male and female. God is so wonderful. He set things up so that the relationship between God and man is intended to be expressed through the relationship between male and female. In this way, what is unseen can be understood through what is seen. The Bible refers to Jesus as the Bridegroom and the church as His bride. God is giving us an earthly and physical illustration to communicate the spiritual truth of our relationship and unity with Him. Therefore, we need to appreciate our creation as males and females, designed specifically for God's love and His purposes in this world. *"For we are God's workmanship, created in Christ Jesus to do good works, which God prepared in advance for us to do"* (Ephesians 2:10).

THE WOMAN WAS PLACED IN THE GARDEN

Fifth, a woman is unique because God specifically placed her in the Garden of Eden along with the man. In Genesis 3:8, we read that God walked in the Garden in the cool of the day in order to meet with Adam and Eve. The Garden represents man's relationship with God, the place of fellowship. A woman cannot fulfill her purpose unless she is in relationship with God. You cannot be the kind of woman you are supposed to be outside of God, any more than a man can be anything outside of God. Any woman who is outside a relationship with the Lord is a dangerous woman, just as a man who is outside a relationship with the Lord is dangerous. You can be who you were created to be, and you can fulfill the purpose you were meant to fulfill, only as long as you remain in the garden of fellowship with God.

> A WOMAN CANNOT FULFILL HER PURPOSE UNLESS SHE IS IN RELATIONSHIP WITH GOD.

A female cannot become what God intended unless she is filled with the Holy Spirit, submits to the Word, and begins to follow the leading of the Spirit. Many of the women of today are not living godly lives. They are not in the garden; they are in the wilderness. Many men are in the same situation.

Do you remember what happened when Adam and Eve rebelled against God? What did God do? He put them out of the Garden. A garden is a specifically manicured, prepared place. Outside the garden is wilderness. Wilderness people are wild; they devour one another. God wants us to be transformed by the renewing of our minds and to get out of the wilderness. (See Romans 12:2.)

You need an ongoing, intimate relationship with God in order to become the woman you were created to be. You can't just read popular women's magazines or watch talk shows and expect to get revelation from God. These sources are usually headed deeper and deeper into the wilderness. They're leading you into perversion and depravity. The wilderness mentality of women is, "I don't need anybody else. I'm going to make it on my own. I don't care what anyone says; I don't need any man." God says that's wilderness talk. I believe you know that's wilderness talk because, deep inside, you have a garden desire. You need to be in relationship with God, and you need to be in relationship with men—with a husband or with your brothers in the Lord—in order to be what you were created to be.

This is the ideal, and God wants you to work back to it. He wants you to have the spirit of the Garden so that you will be in continual fellowship with Him. Then you will be able to experience fulfillment both as a spiritual being created in God's image, and as a female, created for good God's purposes.

You are God's good idea, and His unique creation.

PRINCIPLES

1. A woman is God's idea.

2. A woman's uniqueness is a reflection of God's purposes and design for her.

3. The woman has a spirit within her, making her a free and responsible spiritual being.

4. When you don't treat a woman right, you have interfered with the spirit-man in the female.

5. The female was taken out of the male.

6. The woman needs to stay connected to her source.

7. A husband should love his wife as he loves himself.

8. The head of the man is Christ, the head of the woman is the man, and the head of Christ is God.

9. Christ is our model of submission.

10. A woman isn't less than her husband, but for God's purposes, it is her position to submit.

11. Submission activates heaven.

12. The man is the woman's covering.

13. The source is responsible for the product.

14. The woman was made for everything the man has.

15. In the spiritual realm, there is no difference between men and women; but in the physical realm, there has to be the proper relationship of submission.

16. The woman is "weaker" than the man: delicate, sensitive, and absorbent.

17. The woman was made physically different from the man so that she can bear the offspring of the race.

18. If you are not sure whether you are a female or a male, the evidence is in your physical design.

19. The relationship between God and man is intended to be expressed through the relationship between male and female.

20. The woman was placed in the Garden along with the male.

21. A woman cannot fulfill her purpose unless she is in relationship with God.

CHAPTER FIVE STUDY QUESTIONS

QUESTIONS FOR REFLECTION

1. If you are a woman, what do you like best about being a female? If you are a man, what qualities do you like best about women?

EXPLORING GOD'S PRINCIPLES AND PURPOSES

2. There are five significant ways in which the woman is a unique creation by God. What is the first way? (p. 92)

3. What reason did God give for creating the woman? (p. 92)

4. Ultimately, the woman belongs to whom? Why? (p. 92)

5. Galatians 3:28 says that, in Christ, "*there is neither slave nor free, male nor female.*" Because the spirit-man is within the woman, how should the man treat her? (pp. 93–96)

6. What is the connection between our worship of God and our relationships with others—including our spouses and other members of the opposite sex? (pp. 94–96)

7. The woman needs to stay _____ to the man in order to live the life she was created to live. (p. 97)

8. Paul made an important distinction between the _____ _____ of _____ and _____ and the _____-_____ relationship. (p. 97)

9. According to 1 Corinthians 11:3, both males and females are under authority, as is Christ. The head of Christ is _____, the head of the man is _____, and the head of the woman is the _____. (p. 98)

10. What is the basis on which a wife should submit to the authority of her husband? (p. 98)

11. What must a man do before he can exercise authority and headship over a woman? (pp. 100–101)

12. What happens when a woman tries to exercise authority in the spiritual realm when she is not submitted to her authority in the earthly realm? (pp. 101–102)

13. Why did God design the female to be physically different from the male? (pp. 105–107)

14. A woman cannot fulfill her purpose unless she is in
_____ with God. (p. 108)

CONCLUSION

The woman is God's good idea and His unique creation. The spirit-man lives within her and she is a responsible spiritual being before God. In order to fulfill what she was created to be, the woman needs to be in proper relationship and position with God and man in both the spiritual and physical realms.

APPLYING GOD'S PRINCIPLES TO YOUR LIFE

THINKING IT OVER

+ Because the woman was thought of and made by God, she belongs to Him. Therefore, in whatever way you treat her, you are treating God's idea. If you are a woman, have you really recognized the fact that you are valuable and loved by God as His unique creation? In light of this truth, do you treat yourself with respect? If you are a man, do you value your wife, mother, sister, and other women as belonging to God in a special way?

+ Have you allowed your level of education, job prestige, or salary to affect the amount of love and respect you give to your spouse, who may or may not be "equal" to you in these areas?

PRAYING ABOUT IT

+ Ask God to show you whether you are under authority in both the spiritual and earthly realms. Then read Philippians 2:6–8 and meditate on Christ's equality with and submission to God the Father. Ask God to give you the heart and mind of Christ in relation to submission, whether you are a woman or a man.

+ If you are trying to worship and serve God while not forgiving others or living in right relationship with them, ask God to forgive you, and reconcile with others, so you can worship Him *"in spirit and in truth"* (John 4:24).

ACTING ON GOD'S TRUTH

+ The relationship between God and man is meant to be reflected through the relationship between male and female. Below, write down several ways you can better demonstrate this purpose in your relationship with your spouse or other members of the opposite sex. How will you put these ways into practice in your life?

- No one can fulfill his or her purpose while neglecting to maintain a relationship with God. Are you connected to your Source? Commit to daily fellowship with God and seek Him while making important decisions in your life.

The woman is the result of God's idea,
and that makes her very valuable to Him.

SIX

THE WOMAN AS ENHANCER

Women have one advantage over men.
Throughout history they have been forced to make adjustments.
The result is that, in most cases, it is less difficult for a
woman to adapt to new situations than it is for a man.
—Eleanor Roosevelt
You Learn by Living

In the next three chapters, we are going to explore some specific purposes for which God created the female. If you are a woman, I believe these chapters are especially going to encourage you. You're going to understand more about yourself and why you are the way you are. You're going to learn how to be fulfilled by living according to God's design.

I believe these chapters are also going to be a blessing to men who take to heart the principles in them and apply them in their relationships with women. If you are a man, read these chapters carefully so that, in all your interactions with the woman, whether she is your wife, friend, fellow employee, or even mother, you will be able to assist her in properly understanding and fulfilling her purpose in creation. If you don't know why a woman is the way she is, you will continue to misunderstand and misuse her. The purpose of this book is to bring the knowledge of who the woman is to light, so that she will not be devalued or abused. Both women and men will be able to secure a better relationship with anyone they encounter if they understand and apply the truths in these chapters.

(Please keep in mind that these principles reflect the ideal of God's purposes in creation. We haven't yet arrived there, but God wants us to strive for this ideal.)

Many men are having problems in their lives today for two reasons. First, they don't know their own purpose; second, they definitely don't understand the woman's purpose. When men do not know their own purpose or the woman's purpose, this has a negative effect on the woman, causing her both stress and heartache. Yet when a woman understands her purpose and how it relates to the man's purpose, she

> THE FEMALE HAS BEEN PLACED IN HER POSITION NOT BECAUSE SHE IS LESS IMPORTANT, BUT BECAUSE OF HER FUNCTION.

can bring much healing and fulfillment to her relationships. She may even be able to alleviate some of the situations of misuse and abuse in her life. You'll be amazed at what a woman who knows her purpose can become. I've met very few men who can handle a woman who knows her purpose.

"Many are the plans in a man's heart, but it is the LORD's purpose that prevails" (Proverbs 19:21). Many are the plans, the opinions, the doctrines, and the concepts that are in our hearts, but it is God's purpose that counts. When we rely on our own understanding of our purposes, we run into difficulty. Yet when we understand God's purposes for us, we can address the needs that come with those purposes. In this way, we can live fulfilled lives.

Purpose determines design and also position. We learned in the discussion of authority and submission in the last chapter that a woman has been placed in her position not because she is less important, but because of her function. Men and women have the privilege of being different. These differences are due to their specific roles in exercising dominion over the earth.

This chapter will discuss the woman's dominion role as enhancer. The male, who was created first and was given the role of responsible spiritual leader and visionary, was not meant to live in isolation or to fulfill his calling on his own. As enhancer, the woman is a coleader who shares his vision and works with him to accomplish what they were both created to do. The woman takes who the man is and what the man has and enlarges and extends it. In this way, his leadership is effective and their shared vision becomes reality.

THE WOMAN IS THE MAN'S COMPANION

God always tells you why He makes something before He makes it. *"The LORD God said, 'It is not good for the man to be alone. I will make a helper suitable for him'"* (Genesis 2:18). Therefore, the first purpose of the female as enhancer is to be a companion for the male, so that he won't be alone. The word *alone* is made up of two words, "all" and "one." When you put the two words together, you see that *alone* basically means "all in one."

God said, "It is not good for this male-man to be all in one, having everything in himself." Thus God drew out another self from him, so that the man would have this other self to share with. God made the female so that the male would have someone to give to, someone to share his vision with, someone to be a part of his life. Isn't it sad that many men don't see women in this way? The female was created so that the male would not have to be alone. She is his life companion.

"To companion" means to accompany, to attend, and even to guide someone. It is in this sense that a woman is a man's companion.

THE WOMAN IS GOOD FOR THE MAN

God said, "It is not good for this male-man to be alone." It is clear that, when God made this statement, He meant that what He was about to create for the man would be good for him. Therefore, the Word says, "Women are good. Females are good." The woman was created for the man's good.

I want to say to my women readers that God knew what men needed, and it was you. When something is made for something else, it has within it that which the other thing needs. When something is made to be good for something else, it has that which is good for the other thing. Therefore, everything God created the female to be is good for the male.

A female is very, very good for a male, but where purpose is not known, abuse is inevitable. A woman can abuse her nature and purpose if she doesn't understand why she is the way she is. In addition, a woman who does not understand her purpose can be a detriment to a man, and a man who doesn't understand the woman's purpose can be a detriment to a woman.

Yet God said that the highest good for a man, besides Himself, is a woman. So, in some mysterious way, in spite of what your past experiences in relationships might have been, a woman is, by her very nature, good for a man.

THE WOMAN SHARES THE MAN'S VISION

As enhancer, the woman also enables the man to accomplish the vision and purpose for which they were both created. She shares in this vision, encourages the man along the way, and helps him to accomplish it. If a man has a vision, a woman should do everything in her power to see that it comes to pass.

Women, when you help a man, it doesn't mean you are putting him down or putting yourself down. It means that you both have equal responsibility, each in the proper position.

In Genesis we read that God made the male first, and that He showed him everything that had been created. Then God told the male what to do with the earth. Therefore, the man was given the dominion vision first. It is important to remember that this is God's vision, not just the man's vision. I need to impress upon both female and male that it is necessary for a male to have a vision for himself, his family, and all those under his influence. He must have a vision, for he was created to be a visionary.

After God had given the man responsibility and work in the Garden, and after He had told the man to have dominion over the earth (the vision), then He said, "I'm going to create a helper for the man." Therefore, one of the purposes of the woman is to share in the vision and responsibilities of the male.

A male was not meant to carry out his ministry by himself. His vision was not supposed to be fulfilled by himself. This means that a woman was not made to fulfill a vision by herself, either. Everything that the female has—her talents, gifts,

THE DOMINION ASSIGNMENT WAS GIVEN TO BOTH MEN AND WOMEN.

expertise, experience, and education—was given to her to help the male fulfill God's vision. This is the reason why women have so much talent. The problem is that men and women don't understand their purposes, and so they end up using their talents against one other. The woman uses her talents to prove that she doesn't need the man, instead of using them to help the man. The man hates this use of her abilities because he feels she's intimidating him. When this happens, both of them lose their purpose in life, and both of them are dissatisfied, because she can't fulfill her purpose without him, and he needs her to help him fulfill his purpose. They need each other, but they end up working against each other.

What vision did God give to the man? He said, "Here's the Garden: subdue it, work it, cultivate it. Make it better than it is. Develop it, and produce more of it." In other words, "Take this planet and make it richer than it is. There is seed in this ground that hasn't yet born fruit. Make it a harvest. There is gold in the mountains. Dig it out. There are diamonds in the rough. Mine them. I'm going to send you a helper to get this done."

Again, the dominion assignment was given to both men and women. This means that the woman is meant to help the man fulfill this vision in all areas of life. However, when the man sees the woman coming into the corporate office, he becomes jealous. "What's she doing here?" he says. "Her place is in the home." Where did that idea come from? It did not come from God. This beautiful, precious gift of the woman was given to men so that they wouldn't be alone. Yet do you know what men do to women? They despise the very thing that was given to them for companionship and help. Woman were made to share the man's vision and to help him fulfill it.

One of the ways a woman can help the man to fulfill the vision is to give him respect. *"Each one of you also must love his wife as he loves himself, and the wife must respect her husband"* (Ephesians 5:33). The woman is meant to bless, support, and honor the man, and the man is meant to be a head, a covering, and a protection for her. In this way, they are helping each other to be all they were created to be. Yet these purposes break down when the man and the woman don't know each other's needs.

For example, a man always wants to feel as if he has had some input into what has been accomplished; he wants to feel as if he is a leader. If you are a wife, try to make your husband feel that he has contributed significantly to your family's success. When you make a man feel that he is important to what has been accomplished—that he is the one responsible for, or that his input was necessary for, the success of something—then you will have somebody who serves you, because a man feeds on respect. However, if you make him feel unimportant, you will run into trouble. "Well, I don't need you anyway; I've already been doing this for ten years without you." When you communicate that kind of idea to a man, he will back further and further away from you. He may even go elsewhere, to someone who believes he is everything. That's the person he will stay with, or move in with, because that's the person who is fulfilling the needs of his hungering soul.

A man needs respect. This means that the worst thing you can do is to compare your husband to another male. Please don't tell your husband, "Why can't you be like our pastor?" or, "Why aren't you like So-and-so?" That's the most dangerous—and ridiculous—thing a woman can say to a man. Every man is his own being and has his own image of himself. Your job is to support him, even if he is not perfect, and to be an encouragement to him. You have to learn his nature and understand him. The eyes of the woman must be looking to the needs of her husband.

THE WOMAN IS THE MAN'S HELPER

According to the Word of God, a woman is also created to be a help-mate. "*I will make a helper suitable for him*" (Genesis 2:18). A woman is a helpful agent for the man. Let me suggest to you that if a woman is meant to be a helper, she has been designed with many qualities and abilities that equip her to help.

The woman's purpose is to assist the man in fulfilling God's plan for his life. The implications of this are profound. First, it means the male has to have a plan; otherwise, the female is in trouble. Second, it means that

> A WIFE AND HUSBAND NEED TO SHARE THE SAME VISION.

the female must understand that her fulfillment is related to the male's vision. In other words, she can never really be complete if she does not help him fulfill his vision. A woman has to think, before she does anything, "Is this a help to the man?" If it is not a help, then she is abusing her purpose.

When a wife decides she wants a completely different vision for her life than her husband's vision, they will experience a di-vision. *Di* means two or double. The word *division* could be thought of as "double vision." Whenever you have a couple who has double vision, they are in danger of divorce, because "*a house divided against itself will fall*" (Luke 11:17). You can't have two visions in the same household, or the man and the woman will be going in different directions. That is why God created the woman to be in a helping position. Helpers don't take over; rather, they assist. This certainly does not mean that a woman should not have her own interests and develop her own abilities. It means that, as a couple, they need to share the same vision for their lives.

As a woman, even though you may be talented, educated, intellectual, experienced, eloquent, and well-dressed, God says, "I gave you all of these things, not only for your own enrichment and enjoyment, but so that you can be a help to men. You need to use these gifts in your position of helper, of coleader." What are you using your gifts for? Are you using them to prove to the man that you are just as good as he is? That's not a help; that's competition.

The woman sometimes needs to exercise extra wisdom when helping the man, because the last thing many men want women to believe is that they need their help. They do not understand how God has designed women to help them. God has said that the man needs the woman's assistance. Yet when she starts helping, sometimes the man interprets her help as nagging. For instance, imagine a man who is not doing what he's supposed to be doing in his home. His wife says to him, "Sweetheart, you aren't praying. You didn't pray over the food. We didn't read the Word today." Can't you hear his *ego* screaming, "I'm going to tell you what to do in this house; I'm the man in this house; I'll pray when I'm ready"?

The helper is just trying to help him. She's trying to say, "Look, God's vision is for you to be the spiritual leader for me and for our children; however, you can't be spiritual if you won't develop your spiritual life." So the next day she says, "When are we going to pray?" He retorts, "Don't bother me right now. The Lord will tell me when to pray." The helper is prevented from doing her job.

Or suppose the woman says, "When are we going to pay the mortgage?" He answers, "I've been thinking about it; let me alone." The next day she says, "The man called about the mortgage." "Never mind!" he says. Now he's really getting angry at his helper, when she is just fulfilling what she was created to do.

I think many of us have been brought up in societies where men don't think they need any help. Therefore, when the helper starts to do what she's meant to do, the man goes completely off his rocker, blows his top, and destroys the gift that's in the helper. The man needs to appreciate the woman's role of helper, and the woman needs discernment when giving help.

For example, if a woman's husband gets fired or laid off, and she says, "Did you lose your job *again?* You're always putting the family in these bad situations," she isn't helping. She is destroying the man's self-esteem, wiping out his self-confidence. She is burying his self-respect while she thinks she's helping. "You know, my mother told me not to marry you. My sisters warned me of this...."

Women, you don't know what words like that do to a man. If the man messes up or falls down, don't kick him. Helpers pick people up and dust them off. When they fall down again, they pick them up again. Do you know how many men are where they are today because the helper made sure they got there? Whatever the man is not, it is the woman's job to help him become. He might not yet be the best husband, he might not yet be spiritually mature, but it is your job to help him.

If the man you are married to loses his job, he will need much understanding and support. He will need someone who embraces him and says, "It's okay, honey. It doesn't matter about money or anything else.

> A WOMAN CAN HELP A MAN GREATLY IN HIS SPIRITUAL LIFE.

You're still mine. We could live in a hut and be happy. The book of Proverbs says that it's better to be happy with a little morsel of meal than to eat steak in contention. I would rather move back into a one-room apartment and be with you than live in some mansion without you. We'll be happy in Jesus, because you're still my man. You're God's covering for me." If you want to see a man run right out and look for another job, say something like that—with sincerity. Women don't know the power God has given them to bless men.

A woman can also greatly help a man in his spiritual life. If your husband doesn't pray, don't say, "You don't pray." Instead, pray *for* him. That is a way you can really help him. Then encourage him whenever he shows an interest in spiritual matters. Don't make him feel as if he's not spiritual.

I've seen some women who do not know how to help their husbands after their husbands receive the Lord. For example, a woman prays for her husband for twenty years, and he finally becomes a Christian. He goes to church with her, and she praises God for this answered prayer. Then, all of a sudden, she becomes depressed. I've seen this happen time and time again. Why does she become depressed? Perhaps her husband hears a statement from the Scriptures, or he hears someone in the church say something about God, and he asks, "Where is that found in the Bible?" She overhears him asking this and feels bad because he isn't yet an expert on the Bible. Or, maybe he prays a little too loudly during the prayer meeting, and she feels ashamed because she thinks he doesn't know how to conduct himself. The best thing she can do to help him is to let him ask his questions, let him learn to pray, and be thankful about the wonderful things God is doing in his life.

Or perhaps a woman sees her newly converted husband reading the Bible, and she says, "Why don't you take the garbage out?" She's not helping. The garbage can wait a little while longer. She should let him read. There may also be some jealousy involved. She might say, "Now that you're saved, you sit and read the Bible for three hours at a time. Do you think you're more spiritual than I am? All you talk about is church, church, church." Instead, she should say, "I'll help you take the garbage out, honey." Why? She will be helping him to become the spiritual leader of the home, and this will be a blessing to her. Many men try to move close to God, but their wives push them away from Him. Instead, they need to help support their husbands' spiritual growth.

Many men are put off by their helpers, because they are made to feel very uncomfortable. Helpers are supposed to make people feel comfortable. A man cannot receive help from a woman who is antagonistic against him. He cannot receive help if she is offended by him. Under those circumstances, he needs all his power to maintain his purpose.

To help means to assist. Whenever the female decides that she is tired of helping and is now going to become the boss, her home is in trouble, her relationship is in trouble.

In Genesis we read that God told Abraham he was going to have a son. When the promise was delayed, his wife, Sarah, thought she would try to help her husband by giving him her maid as a concubine so that they could have a child through her. She was trying to help her husband, but she was trying too hard. God wanted Sarah to be the mother of the child. She should have helped by believing God and receiving the promise in God's timing. Instead, she created heartache and strife for herself and her husband. (See Genesis 16 and 21.)

There is another point about the woman as helper that we need to keep in mind. When God said He would make a helper for the man, I believe that He intended the woman to be the *"help meet"* (Genesis 2:18 KJV) for men in general, not just for her husband. This means that, if you are a woman, you are meant to be a spiritual help and encouragement to the men you encounter in life. Please under-

> SOME MEN JUST NEED A GOOD WORD FROM A GOOD WOMAN.

stand that I am not saying a woman has to submit to other men as she submits to her husband; rather, I am saying that she can be a tremendous influence for good in men's lives. Moreover, the helping nature of a woman can be exercised whether a woman is married or single, since it is a natural part of her makeup. A single woman has much to contribute in this way, and if she marries, she can bring into her marriage this valuable experience of exercising her gift and understanding the nature and needs of men.

If you see a man you know destroying his life with drugs, you can go to him and say, "God has so much potential inside of you. It breaks my heart to see you on drugs." Your saying that will be helping him. You don't have to be married to give that type of help. Some men just need a good word from a good woman. Some men don't have good mothers. They have been told negative things about themselves all their lives. They are looking for a woman to tell them something positive about themselves. Let me caution you that this can require careful discretion on the woman's part so that the wrong impression is not given. Yet a woman can be a powerful force for good in a man's life by being an encouragement to him.

Yes, men are starving for good words from women, especially Christian women. Yet sometimes Christian women are the ones who destroy men the most because they misunderstand their priorities in God. They say, "God comes first," and so they neglect their families. The Bible uses strong words about such behavior. It says, *"If anyone says, 'I love God,' yet hates his brother, he is a liar. For anyone who does not love his brother, whom he has seen, cannot love God, whom he has not seen"* (1 John 4:20). I'm referring to women who go out to save the world but lose their families. They need to think carefully about the help they give. Instead of staying away from home every night of the week to attend prayer meetings, they should be finding ways to encourage and help their husbands and families. That is the way they can best love God.

THE WOMAN IS ADAPTABLE TO THE MAN

God said, *"I will make a helper suitable for him"* (Genesis 2:18). Another word for *suitable* is *fit*, which means "adapted to an end or design." A woman is designed for the purpose of adapting to the man. This means that she has the built-in energy and the built-in circuits to adapt to his vision and purpose.

Consider the following illustration. A plant grows from the soil and has to stay rooted in the earth in order to live. What determines the health of the plant? The soil that it's in. If you plant it in soil that is full of nutrients, it will likely thrive. Yet if you plant it in soil that is high in salt content, it will become sickly and might even die. So the plant adapts to what it receives from the environment to which it is connected. Therefore, based on the quality of the soil from which the plant comes, you can usually determine the health and the nature of the plant.

God said, "I'm going to make a creation from man that will adapt to the nature of the source from which she comes. Whatever the man feeds her, she will become like that." If you take a plant and put it in red-dyed water, the plant will absorb the color, and it will show up in the leaves or blossoms. A similar thing happens in the life of a woman. A woman adapts herself to the source from which she came, the male, and absorbs nourishment from him. Therefore, if the man doesn't like the woman's colors, so to speak, he needs to change the water that he's giving his plant. If the man doesn't like the way the woman is manifesting herself, then he has to check to see what kind of nutrients—or what kind of poison—he is feeding his wonderful plant.

A woman's adaptability also means that if a woman enters a situation or environment, she is more prone to become like it than the male is. This trait can be a tremendous blessing, but it can also be dangerous. This is why women have to be careful not to open themselves up to any and every environment.

A female is more emotional than a male because she is moved by environmental stimuli. Therefore, a woman will become excited when, for the first time, she enters a church service in which the Spirit of God is very strong. A man will walk in with her at the same time, sit in the back, and check it out. If she is asked if she would like to join the church, she will join in three weeks; he will join in three years.

The man is different from a woman. He is wired to be logical, so he wants a logical explanation for everything. "Why do you raise your hands?" he will ask. "You can worship with your hands down." "Why do you always sing in that funny language?" "It's a gift of the Spirit." "Do I need to speak in tongues?" "Not necessarily, but it is good because it edifies you." On the other hand, a woman will generally say, "This is great. I want it, whatever it is." She's reflecting her purpose.

Do you wonder why there are usually more women than men in the churches? It is because of the way they're made. A woman will always submit and adapt more easily to spiritual things because of her purpose, because of the way she is designed. Most of the time, it takes men a long time to become logically convinced.

Now, it's hard for a woman to adapt to someone who isn't leading. She cannot follow someone who isn't going anywhere. She cannot adapt to the man who doesn't know what he's doing. The woman can't function properly if the man doesn't function. Therefore, if a man wants a woman to adapt to him, he has to give her something to adapt to. There are many men walking around who have nothing to do, and they're asking women to help them with it. That's illegal. God told the man, "You will be a provider. You will provide the vision." A man was made to have a vision. A female was made to help him fulfill it. But if he doesn't have a vision, how can she help him? She can't help a man do nothing.

> THE WORLD IS FILLED WITH FRUSTRATED FEMALES WHO ARE LIVING WITH MEN WHO AREN'T GOING ANYWHERE.

The world is filled with frustrated females who are living with men who aren't going anywhere. It's ridiculous for a man to ask a woman to leave her parents' home to follow him when he isn't going anywhere. The first question a woman should ask a man when he asks her to follow him is, "Where are you going in life?" If he can't answer this question, she should tell him to find a map and say that she'll talk to him later. A woman is too precious to waste sitting in a house being frustrated for twenty years. It breaks my heart to see the precious, awesome potential of females being suffocated by some male who doesn't know what he's doing. God says, "I created her to adapt to the male." Yet the male has to have something for her to adapt to.

It's difficult enough to have nothing to adapt to, but it's even worse if you have to adapt to something that isn't right for you. Many men want women to adapt to a lifestyle that they themselves feel is contrary to their own convictions. The word "adapt" could be translated "submit." The woman is wired to submit, but she should truly submit only when she recognizes the man's moral authority over her.

Some men don't deserve to be adapted to. They are not worthy of it. They're not giving the adapter that which is comfortable to adapt to. When this is the case, you will find women adapting in bitterness, in hatred, in deceit, or in malice. They're being forced to adapt to something against their wills, and they hate it.

Whatever the male gives off or gives out, the female will generally adapt to. Eventually, she may become it. She was born to adapt, she was designed to adapt, and so she becomes whatever she feeds on. I have observed women whose husbands or boyfriends are prone to swearing. These women, likewise, eventually develop the habit of swearing. Children also have their roots in the soil. They suck up whatever is coming from their source, and they end up producing the same kind of fruit as their source. In this way, you end up with a family that looks just like the father. The cause of this is adaptability.

Why do you think many women are now smokers? Years ago, there was a cigarette advertisement that featured a tall, slender woman who had a long cigarette in her hand and was smiling. The only healthy look about her was her teeth. The caption across the top read, "You've come a long way, baby."

That advertisement was saying, "You men had your cigarettes for a long time. Now we've adapted, and we have ours." Women can adapt to anything. Men started smoking dope, shooting up, and taking crack; then, women said, "Well, let's adapt." Now we have as many females as males, maybe even more, taking drugs. Why? They have adaptable circuits; they are vulnerable.

A woman has a tremendous spirit of adaptability. I've heard men say, "If my wife did to me what I do to her, I'd have been gone a long time ago." They are saying that there is something about women that makes them able to stay longer in an uncomfortable situation than men would. The reason is this spirit of adaptability. "He beats me, but I've adapted to it." "He sleeps around, but I've adapted to it." "He takes all our money and gives it away, but that's okay. I still love him; I've adjusted to it." "He comes in late and sleeps in twice a week, but God's good; I'll adapt to it. I'm getting used to it."

Yet while a woman is designed to adapt, she isn't designed to adapt forever. Remember what we learned in an earlier chapter? Women have a tremendous ability to allow things, but they won't allow abusive behavior to go on forever. Even though women may be submissive in spirit, they're not stupid. Even though they may be prone to put up with things because of their adaptable spirit, they're not designed to put up with things indefinitely. Love may suffer long, but only long—not forever. There comes a time when the adapter runs out of adaptation. The woman reaches a point at which she needs to adapt to some freedom and find something worthy of spending her life on. A man must be careful that he treats this spirit of adaptability with care and sensitivity, and considers it as a valuable aspect of his unity with the woman.

THE WOMAN ENHANCES HER OWN LIFE

The woman is therefore an enhancer by being a man's companion, being good for him, sharing his vision, being his helper, and being adaptable to him. In all the ways in which the woman enhances the man's life, she is also enhancing her own, since she is a coleader and participant in the dominion vision that was given by God to the spirit-man. When a woman and man learn to live together harmoniously within their purposes and positions, helping and supporting one another, they can live the life they were created to live and find lasting contentment and fulfillment.

PRINCIPLES

1. In the woman's dominion role as enhancer, she is a coleader with the male. She shares his vision and works with him to accomplish what they were both created to do.

2. The woman takes who the man is and what the man has and enlarges and extends it. In this way, his leadership is effective and their shared vision becomes reality.

3. The first purpose of the female as enhancer is to be a companion for the male, so that he won't be alone.

4. The second purpose of the female as enhancer is to be good for the male.

5. The third purpose of the female as enhancer is to share the man's vision.

6. The woman enables the man to accomplish the vision and purpose for which they both were created.

7. One of the ways a woman can help the man to fulfill the vision is to give him respect.

8. The fourth purpose of the female as enhancer is to be the man's helper.

9. When a wife decides she wants a completely different vision for her life than her husband's vision, they will experience a division.

10. When the female decides she is tired of helping and is now going to become the boss, her home is in trouble.

11. God intended the woman to be the helpmeet for men in general, not just for her husband.

12. The fifth purpose of the female as enhancer is to be adaptable to the man.

13. A woman adapts herself to the source from which she came.

14. If a woman enters a situation or environment, she is more prone to become like it than the male is.

15. A female is more emotional than a male because she is moved by environmental stimuli.

16. Whatever the male gives off or gives out, the female will generally adapt to.

17. In all the ways in which the woman enhances the man's life, she is also enhancing her own, since she is a coleader and participant in the dominion vision.

CHAPTER SIX STUDY QUESTIONS

QUESTIONS FOR REFLECTION

1. Do you agree with Eleanor Roosevelt that it is less difficult for a woman to adapt to new situations than it is for a man? Why or why not?

EXPLORING GOD'S PRINCIPLES AND PURPOSES

2. What is the first purpose of the female as enhancer? (p. 118)

3. "To companion" means to _____, to _____, and even to _____ someone. (p. 118)

4. God said that the _____ _____ for a man, besides Himself, is a _____. (p. 118)

5. List an important way that a woman can help a man to fulfill the vision. (p. 120)

6. Why is it inappropriate for a woman to compare her husband with another male? (p. 121)

7. What are two implications of the woman's purpose of assisting the man in fulfilling God's plan for his life? (p. 121)

8. When a wife decides she wants a completely different vision for her life than her husband's vision, they will experience a _____-_____. (p. 121)

9. Why can't there be two separate visions in the same household? (pp. 121–122)

10. In what ways can a woman's helping nature be exercised in the lives of the men she encounters in her daily life? In what ways is this helping different from and similar to her help and support for her husband? (p. 125)

11. A woman has the _____-_____ _____ and the _____-_____ _____ to _____ to a man's vision and purpose. (p. 126)

12. If a man doesn't like the way a woman is manifesting herself, what should he do? (p. 126)

13. What is one reason the female is more emotional than the male? (p. 127)

14. Why is it important for the man to have a vision and to know where he is going in life? (pp. 127–128)

15. What is the woman doing at the same time she is enhancing the man's life? (p. 129)

CONCLUSION

The woman is an enhancer by being the man's companion, being good for him, sharing his vision, being his helper, and being adaptable to him. The man must be careful to treat the woman's spirit of adaptability with care and sensitivity, and consider it a valuable aspect of his unity with her. When a woman and man learn to live together harmoniously within their purposes and positions, helping and supporting one another, they can live the lives they were created to live and find contentment and fulfillment.

APPLYING GOD'S PRINCIPLES TO YOUR LIFE

THINKING IT OVER

+ Have you been comparing your spouse (or another family member) unfavorably with someone else, or have you been helping your mate to become all he or she was created to be in his or her own uniqueness?

+ If you are a woman, are you willingly exposing yourself to situations and environments that are spiritually or emotionally unhealthy for you? If you are a man, are you creating a negative environment in your home to which your spouse or other female family members are having to adapt? If so, what steps will you take to change the situation?

PRAYING ABOUT IT

+ Women often don't know the power God has given them to bless men. If you are a woman, pray for your husband's spiritual life or the spiritual lives of other males in your family, church, or community. Ask God to give you words of spiritual encouragement for them.

+ Have you perhaps been neglecting your family for the purpose of "serving" God? Ask God to show you how you can better minister His love to your family.

ACTING ON GOD'S TRUTH

+ If you are a woman, before acting or reacting toward your husband or other men, ask yourself, "Will what I say or do be a help or a hindrance?" If it would be a hindrance, then consider what you might say or do to be a help.

✦ God has designed men to be visionaries and leaders. If you are a wife, show your husband respect by enabling him to feel that he has made a significant contribution to your family's success through his advice or direct actions. Support him, even though he is not perfect, and be an encouragement to him. Take time to learn his nature and to understand him, so that you can be looking to the needs of your husband. Below, list what you know or are learning about his nature and needs.

"The LORD God said, 'It is not good for the man to be alone. I will make a helper suitable for him.'"
—Genesis 2:18

SEVEN

THE WOMAN AS REFLECTOR

In this chapter we will discuss a second aspect of the woman's dominion role: her role as reflector. Man, the spirit, was created out of the essence of God and in the image of God in order to receive God's love and to reflect His nature. The female was created in the same pattern. She was made out of the essence of the male and in the physical image of the male in order to receive the male's love and to reflect his nature. The parallels between the creation of the spirit-man and the creation of the female, as we learned earlier, are striking. They have significance for our personal relationships with the Lord and also our representation of the love of Christ to the world. We will first look at the woman's purpose as reflector and what this means for the male-female relationship. Then we will look at the spiritual implications of the church's role in reflecting God's nature to the world as the bride of Christ.

THE WOMAN IS THE OBJECT OF THE MAN'S LOVE

THE WOMAN IS DESIGNED TO RECEIVE LOVE

The single most important reason that the female was created was so that she could receive love. Therefore, the first purpose of the female as reflector is that she was made to be the object of the male's love and to reflect the love that he gives her.

When God made woman, He drew her out of man so that the man would have someone to love who was of his own nature. It was love that brought about the woman's existence. In this way, the man was created to be a giver of love and the woman to be a receiver of love. In the last chapter, we saw how the woman's receiving nature makes her adaptable to the man and to her environment. Yet the *primary* purpose of the female's receiving nature is to receive love.

What this means is that God has designed the woman to function on love. Love is the fuel of a female. When you don't give a car fuel, it can't run. The same thing happens with a woman. If you don't give her the love she is meant to receive, she also can't fully function in the way she was created to. In order to be fulfilled, the woman needs love.

In Ephesians 5, Paul said, "*Husbands, love your wives*" (v. 25). He expressed this thought three times: "*Husbands, love your wives, just as Christ loved the church and gave himself up for her*" (v. 25). "*Husbands ought to love their wives as their own bodies. He who loves his wife loves himself*" (v. 28). "*Each one of you also must love his wife as he loves himself*" (v. 33).

The man should love the woman because she was drawn from him and is a part of him. If he doesn't love her, it is the equivalent of the man hating himself. (See verse 29.) He treats himself well when he treats his wife well. The man's role, then, is to love his wife as himself, with all the attributes of love that are found in 1 Corinthians 13:

> *Love is patient, love is kind. It does not envy, it does not boast, it is not proud. It is not rude, it is not self-seeking, it is not easily angered, it keeps no record of wrongs. Love does not delight in evil but rejoices with the truth. It always protects, always trusts, always hopes, always perseveres. Love never fails.*   (1 Corinthians 13:4–8)

When you give the female-man love, she comes alive. Yet when she receives anything less than genuine love, it is as if she short-circuits. When you don't love a woman, you are abusing her very nature.

It is interesting to note that nowhere in the Bible does God tell the woman to love the man. The woman is instructed to submit to the man, to respect and to honor him. Yet God commands the man over and over again to love the woman. Why? It is because the Fall damaged the male's God-given natural love for the female, so that he wants to rule over her rather than to love her as himself. This is why, as the male is being restored to God's original design through redemption in Christ, he needs to be instructed to love the woman. For the same reason, the female's God-given natural respect for the male was damaged, and that is why she needs to be instructed to respect him. Thus, when God's purposes are restored, peace is reestablished

THE FEMALE WAS MADE PRIMARILY TO BE LOVED BY THE MALE.

between males and females; however, when the fallen nature is allowed free reign, there is discord.

So the female was made primarily to be loved by the male. When Paul said, *"Husbands, love your wives,"* he was saying, in effect, "Husband, above all else, love your wife. Don't worry about other things before that, because you can take care of those things in due course. If you love her, you will take care of many other problems and potential problems in your marriage. When you give her the love she needs, she will function properly, because she was born to be loved."

A woman will reflect the love or lack of love that she receives. When she is loved, she is better able to live a life of joy and peace, even in the midst of difficult circumstances. When she is unloved, it is as if there is a weight on her heart. Any man who violates a woman's need for love is misusing and abusing God's purpose for the woman. *"Husbands, love your wives and do not be harsh with them"* (Colossians 3:19).

THE WOMAN NEEDS TO HAVE LOVE EXPRESSED THROUGH AFFECTION

Women need to have love continually expressed to them through affectionate words and gestures. We will look at this topic again in a later chapter on a woman's emotional needs. Men are basically logical and unemotional in their outlook on life, and they have a tendency to treat women in the same manner. Yet because of the way women are designed, they interpret a man's logical approach as coldness. Men need to learn how to love their wives in such a way that they can understand and receive their love. That is the key. Women have to be able to receive it. It isn't enough for a man to *think* that he is giving a woman love; he needs to learn the ways in which she receives love. He needs to learn how women in general recognize love, and he needs to learn how his wife in particular recognizes love.

For example, a man stands before the minister and the congregation of witnesses on his wedding day, and tells his wife, "I love you. I will cherish you for the rest of my life, until death do us part." Two months pass and his wife asks, "Do you still love me?" He replies, a little surprised, "I told you that two months ago." Two years pass and she asks, "Do you still love me?" He will be puzzled and say, "I told you that two years ago." Ten years pass. She says, "You haven't told me you love me in the last ten years." He replies, "Honey, I told you that ten years ago, and it still applies! I'll let you know if I ever change my mind." That's not affection, that's ignorance! A woman functions on love; she needs to hear it expressed often. Many women say that receiving gestures of kindness and affection on a regular basis from their husbands, such as physical affection, notes, and flowers, is what communicates love to them. It is not the expense of the gifts as much as the true thoughtfulness behind them and the consistency of receiving them that makes the difference.

Many men believe that they are expressing proper love to their wives by providing them with the essentials in life, such as shelter, food, and clothing, or by giving them expensive items, such as major appliances, cars, and even mink coats. Certainly, many men give these things out of a motivation of love; however, giving such material items is not the essence of love. Love does not say, "I bought you this house. What more do you want?"

What, then, is the nature of the love a man should show a woman?

A WOMAN IS TO BE LOVED AS CHRIST LOVED THE CHURCH

"Husbands, love your wives, just as Christ also loved the church and gave Himself for her, that He might sanctify...her" (Ephesians 5:25–26 NKJV). If a man is going to love his wife, he has to keep company with Christ. He has to find out how Christ loved His church. It will take a lifetime to study that manual on love! He *"gave Himself for her."* Then He sanctified her.

To sanctify something means to take it away from all else, set it apart in a special place, care for it every day, and value it as a priceless gem. To sanctify something means that you do not allow anything near it that would hurt or destroy it. It is set apart for special use. This means that you don't pass it around. It is not available to entertain other people. *"Husbands, in the same way be considerate as you live with your wives, and treat them with respect"* (1 Peter 3:7). When a man really loves his wife, he considers her the crème de la crème. When she receives such love, she will reflect it in her countenance, the way she looks at life, and in her interactions with others.

These principles of a woman's need to receive love have mainly been expressed in the setting of the marriage relationship. However, they can be more broadly

A MAN CAN HELP BUILD A WOMAN'S SELF-ESTEEM.

applied. Just as we talked about how women can be a spiritual help and encouragement not only to their husbands but also to other men they encounter in their lives, men can do the same for women. They can help build a woman's self-esteem by valuing her and treating her with kindness and Christian love. Women need the affirmation of men, just as men need the respect of women. This is particularly important for men to understand, since they are often in positions in authority over women—in the church, in the workplace, and in other realms of life—and they influence their perspectives and attitudes.

We can return to 1 Corinthians 13 as the man's guide to respecting and affirming women in any interaction or relationship he has with them. Men need to remember that females who are under their authority or supervision need to be treated with consideration so that the nature that God has given them will not be quenched. Women often reflect the manner in which they are treated by men; if men reflect the love and nature of Christ in their dealings with women, the women also can reflect the love and nature of Christ.

THE WOMAN REPRESENTS THE NATURE OF THE MALE

The second purpose of the female as reflector is to represent the nature of the male. She is to reflect the essence of all that God created the man to be in His image.

First Corinthians 11:7 says that the woman is the glory of the man. *"A man ought not to cover his head, since he is the image and glory of God; but the woman is the glory of man."*

When we think of glory, we often think of a cloud filled with light. Yet glory in the sense that we are talking about here has to do with the nature of something. Remember our discussion in an earlier chapter about how the sun, moon, and stars have their own kind of splendor or glory? In its larger meaning, the word *glory* can be ascribed to every single thing. The glory of something is its best expression of itself. One of the definitions of glory is "a distinguished quality or asset." You can see a flower in its true glory when it is in full bloom. You can see a leopard or a lion in its true glory when it is at its prime strength. You can see the sun in its true glory at twelve noon. After that, its light begins to fade. The glory of a thing is when it is at its full, true self. Therefore, glory refers to the manifestation, or the exposure, of the true nature of something.

"For God, who commanded the light to shine out of darkness, hath shined in our hearts, to give the light of the knowledge of the glory of God in the face of Jesus Christ" (2 Corinthians 4:6). "Whether you eat or drink or whatever you do, do it all for the glory of God" (1 Corinthians 10:31). When the Bible says that humanity is meant to show the glory of God, it does not mean just lifting one's hands and saying, "Hallelujah!" That is praise, but it is not glory in the sense in which we are speaking. Reflecting the glory of God means reflecting His true nature. God's glory is often best manifested when we respond in a Christlike way in a difficult situation. For example, when somebody rubs you the wrong way at your job, God is saying to you, "Let the glory come out now. Let people see what God is like under pressure."

Therefore, the glory of something is the manifestation of its true and best nature.

The female and the male each have a different kind of glory. The male is to reflect the "image and glory of God" (1 Corinthians 11:7), while "the woman is the glory of man" (v. 7). The Word of God is stating a profound truth. Essentially, it means that if you want to know what a man is like, don't look at the man, look at the woman who is reflecting him. This means that, if you don't like the way women are, the responsibility for it falls on the men. The women are reflecting the men. Of course, each individual is responsible before God for his or her own actions. For example, a woman may reflect her own selfishness rather than her husband's kindness. Solomon said, "A wife of noble ["excellent" NKJV] character is her husband's crown, but a disgraceful wife is like decay in his bones" (Proverbs 12:4). This verse shows the powerful influence a woman can have in a man's life. Yet men have a great responsibility to truly reflect the image and glory of God so that this can be reflected to the women in their lives, and so that the women can reflect God's glory in turn.

I have noticed that when a man gets married, he often reveals what kind of man he is by what his wife is like. If you are a woman who has an interest in a man and want to know what he is really like, don't ask his father or

YOU CAN TELL WHAT THE MEN IN OUR SOCIETY ARE LIKE BY OBSERVING THE WOMEN.

his brothers; talk to his sisters and his mother. My wife did that. Usually, when a man's mother has a good report about him, he's okay. The Bible says it is unnatural for a mother to forget the baby she has nursed. (See Isaiah 49:15.) God designed a special relationship between a mother and a son. A mother can really identify the basic nature of her son. So, if you want to know what a man is like, talk to the women in his life.

You can tell what the men in our society are like by observing the women. Look at our homes; who is running them? The women are often heading them by themselves. What does this tell you about the man? He is not being spiritually responsible, because he is not fulfilling his purpose and position as head of the household. Look at our children; what is their hope for the future? Many of them are directionless. What do they tell you about the man? He is not providing them with vision. Look at the women; more of them are employed than are the men. What does this tell you about the man? He is not fulfilling his purpose. The female—and often the children, as well—show you what the male is like.

If a man's wife is always depressed, angry, sad, or grouchy, it often means that she is reflecting the treatment she is receiving from her husband. A woman should be able to grow in grace and become a better person as a result of being with her husband.

THE BRIDE OF CHRIST

When we look at the spiritual aspects of these principles, we see that Jesus also has a bride who is meant to reflect His nature. In the original Greek, her name is *ekklesia*. The English translation of this word is "church." Jesus sent the church into the world to be a reflection of Himself. He said to His bride, "The world will know who I am and that I was sent by the Father by the way in which you act, by your unity with one another. The world isn't going to come to Me to find out what I'm like; the world is going to come to the bride. If you don't love one another, they'll never know what I'm like." (See John 13:34–35; 17:21–23.)

Do you know why the people of the world aren't coming to Jesus as much as they should? It is because the church as a whole is often a terrible witness, and it is because individual marriages aren't reflecting God's glory. We are not living in the love and unity that Christ said would reveal His nature to the world. Therefore, while the church is to reflect Christ as His bride, it often does not do so. The Bible tells us that this is unnatural. Jesus is the perfect husband and deserves to have His true nature reflected in His bride. The glory of the Lord is meant to be in the church.

REFLECTING GOD TO THE WORLD

And we, who with unveiled faces all reflect the Lord's glory, are being transformed into his likeness with ever-increasing glory, which comes from the Lord, who is the Spirit. (2 Corinthians 3:18)

It has often been said that a marriage is a church within the church. If the world isn't seeing the nature of Christ through the church in the way that it should, per-

> **A MARRIAGE IS A CHURCH WITHIN THE CHURCH.**

haps we should begin to correct this problem by first looking at our homes. We should review the relationships between husbands and wives, fathers and daughters, brothers and sisters. We should then look at the nature of our friendships and the relationships between men and women in the church.

The woman's role as reflector of the man's love and nature can powerfully reveal God's remarkable love for humanity. She can show her family, her community, and the world what it means to be loved by God and to bear the image of the Creator. She can be a witness to the world of God's compassion and sacrifice for man, and of the joy and healing we can receive through His love.

However, the male has a great responsibility in this calling, for if he does not give love that the female can receive and reflect; if he does not reflect the nature of God, then the witness of the family and of the church is greatly weakened.

With the redemption of Christ, the dominion mandate of man expanded to include a mandate for redeemed man—the church—to cultivate the world's people for God. Jesus said to His disciples of those in the world who are lost, *"Open your eyes and look at the fields! They are ripe for harvest"* (John 4:35). If men and women realize the powerful impact of their relationships on the salvation of the world, they will prayerfully and seriously consider how the dominion mandate can be fulfilled as they give and reflect God's love and nature in their day-to-day relationships.

PRINCIPLES

1. The single most important reason that the female was created was so that she could receive love.

2. The first purpose of the female as reflector is that she was made to be the object of the male's love and to reflect the love that he gives her.

3. God has designed the woman to function on love.

4. The Bible tells the man to love the woman, but it does not tell the woman to love the man. It instructs her to submit to and to respect him.

5. A woman will reflect the love or lack of love she receives from a man.

6. Women need to have love continually expressed to them through affectionate words and gestures.

7. Many men believe that they are expressing proper love to their wives by providing them with the essentials in life or by giving them expensive gifts. This does not express true love.

8. If a man is going to love his wife, he has to keep company with Christ. He has to find out how Christ loved His church.

9. A man is to "sanctify" his wife: set her apart in his heart and life and value her as a precious gem.

10. Men are often in positions of authority over women, and they influence their perspectives and attitudes. They should treat the woman with kindness and Christian love so they won't quench her God-given nature.

11. The second purpose of the female as reflector is to represent the nature of the male. She is to reflect the essence of all that God created the man to be in His image.

12. Glory refers to the manifestation, or the exposure, of the true nature of something.

13. The male reflects the image and glory of God, while the female reflects the glory of the man.

14. If you want to know what a man is like, don't look at the man, look at the woman who is reflecting him.

15. Jesus sent the church into the world to be a reflection of Himself.

16. The woman's role as reflector of the man's love and nature can powerfully reveal God's remarkable love for humanity to the world.

CHAPTER SEVEN STUDY QUESTIONS

QUESTIONS FOR REFLECTION

1. What are the qualities of something that is a reflector?

EXPLORING GOD'S PRINCIPLES AND PURPOSES

2. What is the first purpose of the female as reflector? (p. 136)

3. The primary purpose of the woman's receiving nature is to receive love. What happens to a woman when she fails to receive love? What happens when she is given love? (pp. 136–137)

4. When a woman is loved, she is better able to live a life of _____ and _____, even in the midst of difficult circumstances. (p. 138)

5. Many men believe they are expressing proper love to their wives by providing them with the essential material things in life, such as shelter, food, and clothing, or by giving them expensive items or gifts. Yet in what way do women especially need to have love expressed to them? (pp. 138–139)

6. What does a man need to do if he is going to truly love his wife? (p. 139)

7. When a husband sanctifies his wife, how does she reflect this? (p. 139)

8. The principles of a woman's need to receive love apply to women in general, not just to wives. In what ways can a man provide godly affirmation for the women he encounters in his life? (pp. 139–140)

9. If you want to know what a man is really like, what should you do? (pp. 141–142)

10. What can you tell about the men as a whole in our society by observing the women (and children) today? (p. 142)

11. What should a woman be able to do as a result of interacting with her husband or other men? (p. 142)

12. Who is Jesus' bride—the one meant to reflect His nature to the world? (p. 142)

13. Why aren't the people of the world coming to Jesus as much as they could be? (pp. 142–143)

14. What can be done to correct this problem? (p. 143)

CONCLUSION

The woman's role as reflector of the man's love and nature can powerfully reveal God's remarkable love for humanity. She can show her family, her community, and the world what it means to be loved by God and to bear the image of the Creator. She can be a witness to the world of God's compassion and sacrifice for man, and of the joy and healing we can receive through His love.

However, the male has a great responsibility in this calling, for if he does not give love that the female can receive and reflect; if he does not reflect the nature of God, then the witness of the family and of the church is greatly weakened. When men and women realize the powerful impact of their relationships on the salvation of the world, they can prayerfully and seriously consider how the dominion mandate can be fulfilled as they give and reflect God's love and nature in their day-to-day relationships.

APPLYING GOD'S PRINCIPLES TO YOUR LIFE

THINKING IT OVER

+ If you are a man, are you endeavoring to reflect the image and glory of God in your life so that, in turn, they can be reflected in the life of your wife and other women with whom you interact?

+ Are you living in love and unity with other Christians so that you can reflect Christ and be a witness to the world?

PRAYING ABOUT IT

+ Read 2 Corinthians 3:18. Ask God to show you what areas He wants to work on in your life so you may be *"transformed into his likeness with ever-increasing glory."* As He shows you specific areas, commit them to Him and rely on the Holy Spirit to bring about this transformation as you meditate on and obey God's Word.

+ Ask God to reveal to you those whom you need to forgive and extend grace to in order to live in love and unity with your brothers and sisters in Christ and be the witness to the world that Christ desires for you to be.

ACTING ON GOD'S TRUTH

+ If you are a woman who is thinking of becoming engaged or is currently engaged, have you talked to your fiancé's family or pastor about his character, which you will ultimately reflect? If not, consider doing so as you seek God's will for your life and as you learn to understand and come to know the man you are planning to marry.

+ Men are basically analytical and unemotional in their outlook on life, and they have a tendency to treat women in the same manner. Yet because of the way women are designed, they can interpret a man's analytical approach as coldness. Men need to learn how to love their wives in such a way that their wives can understand and receive their love. If you are a husband, write out the attributes of love in 1 Corinthians 13:4–8. Practice showing love to your wife daily using these attributes as a guideline. In addition, ask your wife, mother, or sister how she recognizes and receives love and make a point to show her love in those ways.

"And we, who with unveiled faces all reflect the Lord's glory,
are being transformed into his likeness with ever-increasing glory,
which comes from the Lord, who is the Spirit."
—2 Corinthians 3:18

EIGHT

THE WOMAN AS LIFE-GIVER

It has been said that the pressure exerted on a woman's body during delivery would kill a man. Apparently, the pressure is so heavy that a male's body could not physically hold up under it. This phenomenon sheds new meaning on the verse, *"I praise you because I am fearfully and wonderfully made; your works are wonderful, I know that full well"* (Psalm 139:14). When God created the woman to be able to carry a baby to term and to deliver that baby, he gave her extraordinary capabilities. He built her so that she could do what He had designed her to do. The woman was designed to be able to gestate—to conceive, carry a baby to term, and bring forth this new life into the world. Now, as we will see, God's design for the woman as life-giver goes beyond her physical abilities. It permeates her entire makeup as a female. Therefore, the third aspect of the female's dominion role is that she is meant to conceive, develop, and give new life to or "incubate" what she receives into herself.

THE NAMING OF THE WOMAN

After the Fall, but before the man and woman were banished from the Garden, the man gave the woman a name. *"Adam named his wife Eve, because she would become the mother of all the living"* (Genesis 3:20). The name Eve in the Hebrew is *Chavvah*, and it means "life-giver." It is significant that God did not cause the man and woman to leave the Garden before Eve was named. As was mentioned earlier, her ability to bear children, her role of life-giver, was part of God's original design and is not a result of the Fall in any way.

The woman is essentially a life-giver. She was given the ability to receive the seed of the male and to reproduce after their kind. This is an awesome capability. God gave the female a powerful responsibility in the world.

THE WOMAN FOCUSES HER ENTIRE BEING ON CREATING LIFE

During physical pregnancy, the woman's body undergoes a complete transformation: the lining of her womb thickens in order to create an environment for the new life to develop while it is kept protected, safe, and warm; her hormone levels change to prevent miscarriage; her brain chemistry alters; her nutrients are directed to go first to her unborn baby and secondly to herself; her center of gravity switches so that she can keep her balance while she shares her body with her unborn baby, and many other changes occur. Pregnancy is a remarkable process that shifts the focus and efforts of the woman's entire body to the task of developing the new life within her womb.

> THE WOMAN HAS PHYSICAL, EMOTIONAL, MENTAL, AND SPIRITUAL "WOMBS."

THE WOMAN IS AN "INCUBATOR" BY NATURE

Yet the woman's dominion role of life-giver is not limited to carrying and delivering a human child. We could call her an "incubator," because her very nature reflects her inclination to develop and give new life to things. This purpose for the woman is not surprising, because there is often a reflection of the spiritual in the physical world, as Paul told us in Romans 1.

Since God created the woman's gestational ability as an integral part of her nature, this ability permeates all areas of her life. She has a physical womb, but she also has an emotional "womb," a mental and instinctual "womb," and a spiritual "womb." She brings forth life in all these areas of her makeup. Everything about her is a womb. She receives things into herself, nurtures them until they mature, and then gives them back in fully developed form.

For example, a sperm isn't much use without an egg. An egg uniting with a sperm is what creates human life, and the resulting embryo's cells begin to multiply when it is in the nurturing environment of the womb. What started as a sperm and egg ends up a fully formed human baby. The fetus has developed so that it now has a life of its own. Similarly, the woman takes from the people and the environments around her—especially her husband, if she is married—and creates something entirely new with what she takes in. Many women don't even know that they are blessed with such an awesome purpose.

Everything goes back to the purpose and design of God. The woman's nature is to be a receiver, and that is why she can receive the seed of the man in order to create a new human life. Yet it is not only a matter of receiving, but also of being able to transform what she has received in a remarkable way, that makes her an incubator. A womb will never give back to you just what it has received. It will always take what you have given it and multiply it.

> **WHATEVER YOU GIVE A WOMAN, SHE'S GOING TO MULTIPLY.**

When a woman receives an idea and incubates it, it becomes something greater—something bigger, stronger, more dynamic. There's so much to it that she staggers with the weight of it. Whatever you give a woman, she's going to multiply. If you give her sperm, she'll give you a baby. If you give her a house, she'll give you a home. If you give her groceries, she'll give you a meal. If you give her a smile, she'll give you her heart. She multiplies and enlarges what is given her.

Therefore, if you want to develop anything, bring it to a woman. Do you have the beginnings of an idea or a prayer request? Tell a woman. Most men will tell their ideas to anyone but their wives. Do you have an idea for a business? Tell a woman. When she comes back to you with it, she will say, "Here's your business." She will have the plan and how to go about it, even from whom to get the money. And the plan will work.

THE CREATIVE PROCESSES OF INCUBATION

What exactly do I mean by incubation apart from actual physical gestation? I mean that the woman is gifted with many creative abilities that can assist her loved ones, herself, and the world. A woman incubates in these main ways:

- She sees possibilities and potential.
- She ponders words, actions, and relationships between things.
- She processes words, ideas, needs, and problems.
- She conceives and invents.

+ She develops ideas, plans, and programs.

+ She protects what she has received while it develops.

+ She produces something new from what she receives.

+ She multiplies what she is given.

You could say that the woman is an entire research and development department all in one. In this, she reflects the nature of her Creator who *"gives life to the dead and calls things that are not as though they were"* (Romans 4:17). Just as God created man out of Himself, a woman brings forth new life from within herself.

This gift of being an incubator has two sides to it, however. It can have a destructive side as well as a creative side, when what the woman receives into herself is not healthy for her emotionally, psychologically, or spiritually. We have seen that because the woman is a receiver, she adapts to or reflects the attitudes and actions of those around her. She takes them in and processes them in a way that can be a mystery to a man, who sees life in a more cut-and-dry way.

THE WOMB OF THE EMOTIONS

For example, many men display domineering or antagonistic attitudes toward the women in their lives over long periods of time. A woman can be pregnant with the bitterness that a man has been presenting her for years. At some point, her long-suffering will come to an end and she will be full-term. The woman has received this bitterness. She has been very quiet for years while she has carried her painful baby, so that the man doesn't understand when she suddenly delivers it. She might say, "That's it! I've had it. I want you to leave." The man will say, "What happened? I've been doing just what I have been doing for the last ten years." "Well, that's it; the baby's come. Get out. Take your clothes, everything, and get out of my house." He wonders what has gotten into her, but the baby has been in her for a long time, growing and developing.

> WHATEVER YOU HAVE BEEN GIVING A FEMALE, YOU WILL RECEIVE BACK— IN A DIFFERENT FORM.

For years, I have been teaching men to be careful what they feed women, because it will come back to them—and in a new, stronger form. Whatever you have been giving a female, you will receive back. It will have grown and developed into something you didn't expect. "Here, this is what you gave me," she'll say. "This is the result of what you presented me." Often, the attitude of a woman is really the "baby" that has resulted from what the man has been giving her.

Suppose a man tells his wife during a heated argument, "I wish I had never married you!" The woman becomes angry when she hears it, but she locks herself into her emotional room. The man may have said a thousand words to her during the argument, but just that one sentence went into her heart, penetrating it just as the single sperm out of millions penetrates the egg at conception. Do you know what she does with it? She incubates it. Nine years later, he says to her, "Honey, you're the sweetest thing I ever married." She says, "You didn't think so nine years ago." The woman is still carrying the baby.

Now, men take care of the business at hand, and then they forget about things. So, he answers, "What are you talking about?" Yet she remembers the date, the time, the atmospheric conditions, what was there, who was there, what color dress she was wearing, and what kind of ice cream she was eating. She incubates things.

A man is different because he doesn't have any wombs. If you say to a man, "You're ugly," he'll say, "You're ugly, too," and then he will forget the incident. However, if you tell a woman that, she'll remember it forever.

Single men have to be careful what they say to single women. If a man says to a woman, "Hey, beautiful, you look great," he is probably going to have a baby in a little while. I'm not talking about a physical baby. He will conceive an emotional baby. The woman will tell him, "You told me you loved me." He'll say, "I was only joking." *"Joking!"*

A woman will incubate your words, so you have to guard what you say.

If a man knows that a woman is an incubator, then he can be careful about what he says to her. Suppose a husband tells his wife that he notices she's put on a few pounds. To him, it's just a casual statement, but it becomes something that the woman incubates. All of the sudden he sees her getting up early and jogging when she never jogged before. He wonders what brought this on, but it is because she has conceived his comment.

Every time he mentions it, she becomes more and more under pressure from the thing. Then she begins to become insecure. She starts to feel as if he is looking at other women and comparing her to them. This builds internally until one day she hears him say something nice about another woman. Then, get out of the way, because here comes the baby!

This principle does not only apply to the relationships between husbands and wives or even men and women in general. Women have to be careful what they say to other women, as well. A woman may tell her friend, "Your hair looks a little different today." She just makes a slight comment about the woman's hair, without any intended implication. Yet that isn't the end of the comment. The friend takes that statement home and incubates it, builds it up, and develops it. A couple of weeks later, the friend gives the woman a piece of her mind. We have to be careful what we say to each other.

A woman forgets nothing. Remember the verse we looked at earlier? *"Can a woman forget her nursing child, and not have compassion on the son of her womb?"* (Isaiah 49:15). A man might even forget he had a son, but a woman can be ninety years old and still say about her seventy-year-old son, "That's my baby." She carried him, she gestated him, and, in a sense, she's still gestating him. She still thinks of ways to help him; she still worries about him.

THE WOMB OF THE MIND OR INSTINCT

God never intended a male to live in isolation. It was never His idea for this to happen because God is love, and, by nature, love desires to share. There are some selfish men in the world who don't want to get married simply because they don't want to have to share their money with anyone. When some married men get paid, they hang onto their paychecks very tightly. They always think a woman is after their money. There may be some truth to this. However, the reason why she is after it is that she is wired to receive. The reason why she is wired to receive is that, if the man keeps his money to himself, it will not multiply. A female is an

> A WOMAN CAN BE NINETY YEARS OLD AND STILL SAY ABOUT HER SEVENTY-YEAR-OLD SON, "THAT'S MY BABY."

incubator. She will never give you back just what you gave her, but above and beyond that.

If you give a woman twenty dollars and say, "Sweetheart, I trust you. Please go ahead and invest this in whatever way you think you should." When you look at that twenty dollars again, it will be two hundred dollars, then two thousand dollars, then twenty thousand dollars. Jesus gave His bride eleven apostles, plus the apostle Paul. She's still multiplying what He gave her. She's not going to give Him back just twelve men. She's going to bring Him millions of men, women, and children. The church is taking the seed of the Word and causing it to multiply into millions of souls so that she can present them to God. God is not going to get back just what He gave. He's going to get more, because He gave it to a woman called the church. The woman is like the servant in the parable of the talents who doubled the investment with which his master had entrusted him.

Men need to understand that a woman's nature can be a great blessing to them.

THE WOMB OF THE SPIRIT

Why is it that few men attend prayer meetings? If you go to a prayer meeting, you will find that it is mainly attended by women. I noticed this at my church and started to wonder about it. Then I realized, "It is because women are incubators. If they are presented with an idea, a need, or problem, they will take it to heart and will work through it until they arrive at a solution."

Just as a womb nourishes a fetus during development and an incubator protects premature or sick babies, a woman has a nurturing instinct that can be a powerful source of help and encouragement in the lives of others.

If a man wants something prayed about, he should tell a woman. She will take the circumstance into her spiritual womb, where she meets with God in her inner being; incubate it for months, if necessary; and then bring forth a solution. She won't give up until she receives an answer from God.

Jesus didn't say that it was a man who kept knocking at the judge's door in order to obtain justice. (See Luke 18:2–8.) It wasn't a man who persisted with the Lord Jesus for a healing for her daughter, saying, "*Yes, Lord,...*

but even the dogs eat the crumbs that fall from their masters' table" (Matthew 15:27). The woman is a incubator. She doesn't quit until she's a full nine months pregnant and ready to deliver.

Do you know to whom God first gave the resurrection message? Women. Do you know why He didn't give it to the males at first? They forget too much. He waited until the women arrived. When Mary showed up, He said, "I want to talk to an incubator. I want someone who can take this and never stop talking about it." It was the women who went and told the men. Why? It was because the men had locked themselves in their room. But the women had gone back to the tomb.

If you give a woman at a well a message, she will turn it into an evangelistic crusade team. (See John 4:4–30.)

THE WOMAN GIVES LIFE TO THINGS

A woman was made to give life. This means that if you need some life in your life, get a life-giver. Some men today are walking around trying to be self-reliant, keeping women at arm's length. They don't know the life they are missing.

God made the female to be the life-giver, so that whenever you need to give life to something, she can do it. Have you ever been in the apartment of a man who is living by himself? The colors are drab. Everything is out of place. It looks horrible. People tell

> GOD WANTS TO SET YOU FREE TO DEVELOP THE GIFTS HE HAS PLACED WITHIN YOU.

him, "You need a woman's touch." When the man gets married and his wife moves in, she changes the drab look. She puts up colorful curtains, places flowers around the rooms, puts pictures on the walls, rearranges the furniture, and, in no time, makes it into a beautiful place. When a woman walks into a room, she changes the countenance of that room. She gives life to a place.

Ladies, your husbands might not be able to provide you with a castle right away, but you can take what they provide for you and give life to it. Take the best that they can offer you, incubate it, and give life to it. When you have finished with it, the house will have become a home.

Many women have gifts of incubation but have been so beaten down by life and the hurtful remarks of others that they have rarely used them. They have been told by men and other women that they have nothing to contribute. If this is your situation, I believe that God wants to set you free to develop the gifts He has placed within you and the ideas and visions He will give you. Don't be afraid. God has given you tremendous ability, and you can be a blessing to many as you reflect the nature of your own Creator and Life-Giver.

———

The last three chapters have explored the woman's purposes in dominion as enhancer, reflector, and life-giver. A female is a unique product of God. Men (and women) must understand her value and contributions, and affirm her in the purposes, designs, and roles for which God created her. In this way, male and female can together become the true reflection of their Creator they were meant to be.

PRINCIPLES

1. The third aspect of the female's dominion role is that she is a life-giver.

2. The woman's dominion role of life-giver is not limited to gestating and delivering a human child.

3. The woman is an "incubator," because her very nature reflects her inclination to develop and give new life to things.

4. Her incubational ability permeates all areas of her life. She has a physical womb, but she also has an emotional "womb," a mental and instinctual "womb," and a spiritual "womb."

5. It is not only a matter of receiving, but also of being able to transform what she has received, that makes the woman an incubator.

6. A womb will never give back to you just what it has received. It will take what you have given it and multiply it.

7. A woman incubates in these main ways:

   + She sees possibilities and potential.

   + She ponders words, actions, and relationships between things.

   + She processes words, ideas, needs, and problems.

   + She conceives and invents.

   + She develops ideas, plans, and programs.

   + She protects what she has received while it develops.

   + She produces something new from what she receives.

   + She multiplies what she is given.

8. When a man knows that a woman is an incubator, then he can be careful and considerate about what he says to her.

9. A woman has a nurturing instinct that can be a powerful source of help and encouragement in the lives of others.

10. God wants to set you free to develop the gifts He has placed within you and the ideas and visions He will give you.

CHAPTER EIGHT STUDY QUESTIONS

QUESTIONS FOR REFLECTION

1. What does it mean to nurture someone or something? Do you think women are more gifted at nurturing than men are? Why or why not?

EXPLORING GOD'S PRINCIPLES AND PURPOSES

2. What does the name Eve mean? (p. 150)

3. What is the significance of the fact that Adam named Eve before the fall of mankind? (p. 150)

4. Why may the woman be referred to as an "incubator"? (p. 151)

5. Besides her physical womb, in what three areas of life does the woman have additional "wombs"? (p. 151)

6. The woman is gifted with many creative abilities that can assist her loved ones, herself, and the world. List eight ways in which a woman "incubates." (pp. 152–153)

7. The gift of being able to incubate can have two sides to it. What are they? (p. 153)

8. What happens when a woman receives into herself what is not healthy for her (or what she perceives isn't healthy for her) emotionally? (pp. 153–155)

9. What happens when you entrust money and other material resources to a woman's mental or instinctual "womb"? (pp. 155–156)

10. What happens when you entrust an idea, a need, a problem, or a prayer request to a woman's spiritual "womb"? (pp. 156–157)

11. Read Luke 18:2–8 and Matthew 15:22–28. What main quality did the widow and the Canaanite woman exhibit that corresponds to a woman's being an "incubator"? (pp. 156–157)

12. Why did Jesus entrust Mary and the other women who came to His tomb (see Luke 24:1–10; John 20:1–18) and the woman at the well (see John 4:4–30) with the messages of His resurrection and eternal life through Him? (p. 157)

CONCLUSION

A woman was designed to give life. She has a nurturing instinct that can be a powerful source of help and encouragement in the lives of others. Men and women must understand all of a woman's value and contributions, including her role as life-giver, and affirm her in the purposes, designs, and roles for which God created her. In this way, male and female can together become the true reflection of their Creator that they were meant to be.

APPLYING GOD'S PRINCIPLES TO YOUR LIFE

THINKING IT OVER

+ If you are a man, consider the impact your words can have on a woman— in both a positive and negative way. Knowing that it is a woman's nature to be an "incubator," how can you be more considerate of what you say and how you act toward women?

+ If you are a woman, have you ever taken personally comments by your husband or other men that were never intended to hurt you? Think of how, in the future, you can balance your natural emotional responses with an understanding of a man's more matter-of-fact approach to things.

PRAYING ABOUT IT

+ Dr. Munroe said that many women have been so beaten down by life and the hurtful remarks of others that they have rarely used their gifts of incubation. They feel they have nothing to contribute. If this is your situation, God wants to set you free to develop the gifts He has placed within you and the ideas and visions He wants to give you. Ask God to heal you of your hurt and to correct the false ideas about yourself that you have accepted in the past, so that you can fulfill the wonderful purposes for which He created you.

+ If you have knowingly or unknowingly undermined someone's self-esteem and potential by what you have said or done to them, ask God to forgive you. Seek reconciliation and pray that God will enable the person to become all she or he was created to be.

ACTING ON GOD'S TRUTH

+ Perhaps you are a woman who is waiting for her husband to make more money or for other circumstances to change before you put your creativity and life-giving abilities into your family, your home, or other endeavors. If so, follow the example of Jesus when He fed the five thousand (see John 6:1–13): take what you *do* have, give thanks for it, and ask God to help you create something wonderful out of it that will be a blessing to yourself and others.

The woman is an entire research and development department
all in one.

NINE

UNDERSTANDING THE WOMAN'S COMMUNICATION STYLE

I have seen too much not to know that the
impression of a woman may be more valuable than
the conclusion of an analytical reasoner.
—Sir Arthur Conan Doyle
(as Sherlock Holmes)

God made women and men very different from each other in the way they think, act, and respond. These differences were designed to be complementary and not divisive. Adam and Eve originally lived in harmony with God, and so they were able to live in harmony with one another. They knew how to draw on each other's strengths in communication for the betterment of them both. However, when humanity turned away from God's purposes and broke relationship with Him, the lines of communication between males and females were cut or at least badly frayed. Thus, the differences that were originally designed to correspond to one another now often lead to misunderstandings and conflicts in marriage and in other relationships between women and men.

The chances are very good that you have experienced some of this misunderstanding and conflict firsthand! Handling differences of opinion and avoiding discord are common problems in relationships.

Consequently, how should you conduct yourself when you have been created to function differently from others with whom you live and work? How are you to live harmoniously with a husband or wife whom you love but who processes information and responds in a manner that is totally distinct from the way that you do? How do you make yourself understood and how do you communicate effectively? Most of all, how do you keep from trying to control another person or driving a wedge between yourself and others because of these differences?

Many women and men struggle with these issues. The answer is to understand the purposes and designs of females and males that influence their communication styles. With this knowledge—and some patience and forgiveness—females and males who are seeking God's redemptive

> HOW DO YOU LIVE HARMONIOUSLY WITH SOMEONE WHO IS DIFFERENT FROM YOU?

purposes for their lives can communicate with one another effectively and happily. Perhaps Colossians 3:13 would be a good guiding principle for us as we deal with differences in communication: *"Bear with each other and forgive whatever grievances you may have against one another. Forgive as the Lord forgave you."* When women and men are considerate with one another, they have the basis on which they can develop the mutual love and respect that is crucial to lasting relationships.

Let us now look at the female's communication style and contrast it with the male's style, so that their different perspectives can be understood and appreciated. In this way, they may be brought into the complementary balance that was God's original purpose for them. This balance will be achieved when females and males understand the strengths of each communication style and when they learn to communicate with each other according to the style that the other party can receive and understand.

The following are the basic natures and tendencies of females and males in communication. Of course, there will always be exceptions, depending on the individual. Yet within the variations, the general tendencies usually hold true.

THE WOMAN IS AN "EMOTIONAL FEELER"

God made the woman primarily as an "emotional feeler," while He made the man chiefly as a "logical thinker." First, let's define these terms.

When I say that a woman is an emotional feeler, I am referring to the way in which she processes and thinks about the verbal and nonverbal communication she receives and perceives from the world around her. Because the woman is an incubator, she not only receives thoughts and ideas into her being but also transforms them as she processes them in her emotional, mental, and spiritual wombs. Her communication style reflects this process. When a woman receives information, she assesses it both mentally and emotionally *at the same time*. This is what makes her distinct from the male, who generally uses these functions separately. Why is this so?

Again, purpose determines design. God's creation is remarkable. He actually designed the brains of females and males to be different. The neural pathways between the left and right hemispheres of a woman's brain (both the logical and the emotional sides) are intact. This explains what often puzzles many men: how women are able to do multiple tasks at the same time, rather than having to focus on just one. The woman's brain allows her to process facts and feelings almost simultaneously. Her emotions are with her all the time she is thinking, and this influences her perspective on the world around her as well as what is communicated to her.

In contrast, there are fewer nerves connecting the two hemispheres of the male's brain, so that the logical and emotional sides are not as closely connected. Because of this, he basically needs to "shift gears" to move from his dominant logical side to his emotional side. This is why men, in general, think in terms of facts and in a linear fashion. They think like a straight line—the shortest distance between two points—which gives them the ability to see the goal (the vision) and to focus their energies on reaching it in the most straightforward and direct way.

Women, on the other hand, tend to think more like a grid than a straight line. A woman's brain is designed to pick up many details that men don't "see," things that go beyond the mere facts, such as the personalities, motivations, and feelings of both herself and others. She can perceive, analyze, evaluate, and see relationships between things all at the same time, like x, y, and z coordinates on a grid track a multiple of factors at the same time.

No one person, and no one gender, can look at the world with complete perspective. Therefore, God has designed things so that when the female-man and the male-man work together in unity, they can help one another to see a more balanced picture of life. They weren't meant to understand the world and fulfill their dominion mandate in isolation from one another. For this reason, they have built-in ways of seeing the world that are of benefit to each other. God designed the woman to look at life through an emotional filter and the man to look at life through a logical filter. This does not mean that women do not use logic or that men do not have emotions. They each just have a specific way of looking at the world.

The woman can help the man see aspects of life, which, if overlooked or ignored, can become detours or potholes preventing him from reaching his goal or from reaching it as quickly as he might have. Her peripheral vision keeps him from being blindsided as he single-mindedly pursues his goals and objectives. On the other hand, the man's linear thinking helps the woman not to become so enmeshed in the many layers of her multi-dimensional thinking that she loses sight of the goal and never reaches it. Women and men need each other to chart the best course in life—one that enables them to reach their common goal but also experience their journey in the fullest, wisest, and most rewarding way possible.

Women often have been written off as foolish and inferior by men because they are expressive and show their emotions. A woman does not need to apologize for her emotions. God made her to feel. Males have assumed that their approach is better than the females' approach, rather than complementary to it. They haven't known or understood how and why the woman was created to be an emotional feeler.

FEELING AND THINKING

What communication between women and men comes down to is feeling, thinking, and self-expression. Women and men both feel. Women and men both think. It is their manner of looking at the world and their self-expression that makes the difference. A woman's first reaction will generally be an emotional one followed by a thinking one. The man's first reaction will be a thinking one, but he will also feel.

Because the woman was created to be more attuned emotionally, she feels everything—from the way a person looks at her to what a person is saying or doing. This is a natural response for her, because she was made to feel the world around her and within her.

> WHEN WE DON'T UNDERSTAND PURPOSE, WE BEGIN TO MISINTERPRET MOTIVES.

For example, a woman will be looking forward to a romantic evening with her husband that they had planned. She will prepare the food, set the table, arrange the flowers, maybe even polish the silverware, and then meet him at the door when he comes home. Her husband walks in, says hello, then strides right past her without noticing that she has dressed up. Instead of going to the table, he goes into the living room and says, "I'm going to have dinner in front of the TV while I watch the news." His mind is still in work mode. He is intent on finding out any information that may affect his work and thus his ability to provide for his wife and family. However, because his wife doesn't understand this, she is deeply hurt at his behavior; her first reaction is to feel that he is ungrateful, inconsiderate, and totally heartless. So she goes into the living room and approaches him angrily. He asks, "What's the matter with you?"

At this point, she sees nothing complementary in the way he is designed. When we don't understand purpose, we begin to misinterpret motives. It is this suspicion that creates conflict. This is why understanding purpose and design is so important. Both the woman's reaction and the man's reaction are related to the way they are made. She took his apparent indifference personally, while his mind was preoccupied with what he was thinking so that he did not notice what his wife was feeling.

When women and men understand that the female-man is an emotional feeler and that the male-man is a logical thinker, they can understand how to use their differences for the betterment of them both. The point is that the distinct differences between women and men are meant to be a help to them—not a hindrance or a source of pain. One way of thinking and communicating is not better than the other way, and the inherent differences between the two are not a result of the Fall. The way women and men are designed is for their good. They just need to exercise patience and understanding and to value the other's contribution.

SELF-EXPRESSION

A woman can generally express her feelings and thoughts better than a man can. Most women love to talk because of God's purpose for them. God designed the woman to communicate what is going on in her heart and mind. Because a man talks less than a woman does, he can sometimes give her the impression that he is not doing much thinking. Men think quite a bit; however, they often don't express their thoughts, and when they do, they express only the most salient points because they are interested in facts rather than details.

This is why a man can walk into the house and bypass a beautifully set table his wife has prepared and not say anything about it. The man needs help in switching his focus from linear thinking about his goals and work to an appreciation of the sensory and emotional aspects of life. Then he can notice and appreciate what his wife has done for him. He also needs to learn to articulate what he appreciates and feels. The woman, on her part, needs to understand that when the man walks by her table without saying anything, it doesn't necessarily mean that he is being inconsiderate. It means that he is in a linear frame of mind, because this is his natural mind-set.

DO MEN REALLY HAVE EMOTIONS?

Contrary to what many women believe, men do have emotions. They just don't always express them—either because it is more difficult for them to or because their thinking rather than their emotions is at the forefront of what they are engaged in. It all goes back to purpose. God designed the man with the capacity to focus on the cold hard facts of a situation. Why? It is because he was created first, and in that position was designed to lead. A leader can't afford to base his decisions on emotion, especially in a crisis.

Remember, we are talking about general tendencies. This doesn't mean that a woman can't lead. However, when she does, she often has to balance her emotions with the facts in order to make the best decisions. Moreover, her instincts can serve her well in this capacity.

I have observed that the way a man acts when he receives information from a woman can make her angry. Suppose she says, "The mortgage is due, and we're behind in our payments." He says, "Don't worry about it. I'll take care of it." His wife says, "But you don't understand what I said. We don't have any money, and they're coming to get the furniture!" He replies, "I know. I said I'll take care of it." The woman phones her mother, cousin, and aunt to tell them about her situation, but the man seems almost nonchalant about it. The woman could interpret

SHE IS FEELING; HE IS THINKING.

his response to mean that he doesn't care. Yet all this time, he's been thinking about what he's going to do. She is feeling; he is thinking. He is formulating all kinds of schemes in his head about how he can get the money. Since a female is an emotional feeler, she is generally led or motivated by her emotions, even though she also thinks. Yet a male is led or motivated by his thinking because of his leadership and provider responsibilities.

There are times when a woman isn't feeling what a man is thinking, and a man is not thinking what a woman is feeling. When this happens, the lack of communication between them compounds their frustration with one another. Men need to learn to tell women what they are thinking and feeling. Again, when the man walks past the beautifully laid dinner table, he has to remember to express his feelings. At the same time, the woman shouldn't consider his unemotional response as being either irresponsible or inconsiderate.

A PERFECT BALANCE

The man generally bases his thoughts and actions on what is logical; he factually analyzes everything. This is both a strength and a weakness, because emotions and insights are very important to a person's functioning in the world. Therefore, the man needs someone who can balance his logic with feeling. Otherwise, he'll go through life with merely a cold, logical outlook. He needs someone who can show him the emotional side of life, who can remind him of his need to be sensitive to others. I appreciate God's design. He designed things in such a way that females and males need one another.

The female was created to help the man in that, whatever the male lacks, the female has. The female's emotional feeling will balance the male's logical thinking. Many women don't understand how important they are to the men in their lives. What the male-man lacks, the female-man possesses. The reverse is also true. This principle is based on God's purpose. Whatever God drew out of Adam to make Eve, the man needs in order to be complete. There are qualities in the woman that God took out of the man at creation that a man needs.

WOMEN'S INSIGHT AND DISCERNMENT

There is an interesting example of this truth in the incident where Pilate judged Jesus. Pilate was carrying out his job, the administration of Roman authority over the Jews. When the chief priests brought Jesus before Pilate and accused Him of being an insurrectionist, Pilate's first inclination was to try to rule within the law. He saw no basis for their accusations and wanted to release Jesus. In the middle of this dispute, Pilate's wife sent a warning to him. "While Pilate was sitting on the judge's seat, his wife sent him this message: 'Don't have anything to do with that innocent man, for I have suffered a great deal today in a dream because of him'" (Matthew 27:19). In essence, she was saying, "I have a premonition about this Man. He didn't do anything wrong. Don't touch Him." She was trying to appeal to Pilate's sensibilities, warning him

> GOD GAVE FEMALES TO MALES SO THAT MEN CAN HAVE BALANCE.

that he should use discretion and discernment when making his decision. Pilate became nervous that things were getting out of hand when the religious leaders assembled an unruly crowd to demand that Jesus be crucified. He ended up being swayed by this pressure and ordering Jesus' death. He may have justified his decision by telling himself that it was logical: keeping order for Rome (and making things easier for himself) should take precedence over preserving the life of one innocent man. Even though Pilate knew Jesus had done nothing wrong, he had Him crucified. He would have done better to have listened to the instincts of his wife. Men need to learn to be open to communication from their wives and from the other women in their lives.

God gave females to males so that men can have balance, so that they can have the benefit of women's sensitivity and feeling. It is very easy for men to make a decision and not care what anyone thinks about it or who will be affected by it. This is why it is good for a man to have that other part of him that says, "What you are planning to do may be right, but the way you intend to go about it is wrong. Perhaps you should consider this...."

The account of Abigail in 1 Samuel 25 is a good example of how a woman's discernment averted disaster for a man. Abigail combined intelligence and insight to address a deadly situation. Her husband, Nabal, had rejected David's request for food after David and his men had been honorable with Nabal and had even protected his property. Nabal wasn't using wisdom but his own form of logic and pride when he rebuffed David. (See verses 10–11.) David was angry at the way he was treated and was going to destroy Nabal and the men who worked for him. Abigail went to David and appealed to his sense of justice and righteousness before God and his compassion. Her insights and good judgment kept David from destroying her husband and his men.

Abigail is also a good example of someone who understood how to communicate with another based on a knowledge of the other person's outlook. She knew what to say to David that would get his attention, resonate with his deepest convictions, and get through to him.

MEN'S HEAD-OVER-HEART PERSPECTIVE

Men's logical thinking can also provide balance to women's emotional feeling. There are times when your heart can lead in one direction and your head in another. Sometimes, making the best overall decision requires that you go with your head. If you are a leader during a crisis, you don't have much time to have an emotional experience. You need to be able to think. Our emotions can make it difficult for us to think clearly.

After the Israelites had been freed from Egypt and were approaching the Red Sea, Pharaoh chased after them with his army. When the Israelites saw the Egyptians coming after them, they panicked and accused Moses of luring them to their deaths. Yet Moses exercised leadership when he didn't give in to their panic but rather said, "*Do not be afraid. Stand firm and you will see the deliverance the* LORD *will bring you today. The Egyptians you see today you will never see again. The* LORD *will fight for you; you need only to be still*" (Exodus 14:13–14).

"*You need only to be still.*" Moses was saying, "Instead of letting your emotions control you, instead of running around like chickens with your heads cut off, stay still and trust the Lord." After Moses had gotten everyone under control and everything in order, then he went to talk to the Lord. The man is the way he is because of what he has to do to exercise leadership.

WHAT THE WOMAN SAYS EXPRESSES HOW SHE FEELS

What a woman says is an expression of what she feels, while what a man says is an expression of what he thinks. The woman has thoughts, and the man has feelings. However, a woman will more likely express what she feels, and a man will more likely express what he thinks. They are communicating two completely different levels of information.

THE WOMAN'S HIDDEN THOUGHTS

When a woman is under stress and wants someone to empathize with her so that she doesn't feel so alone in her difficulty, she may say something to her husband like, "Your parents are coming for dinner tomorrow, the house is a mess, we don't have any groceries, the kids have been underfoot all day, and I just can't do it all!" Her husband, who is a thinker, will immediately try to come up with a solution for his distraught wife. "Well, what if I go buy some groceries?" "No, I have to do that tomorrow when I know what I want to cook." "Then why don't I take you and the kids out to dinner so you won't have to worry about that tonight?" "No, we can't be out late. The kids need baths and besides, I have to use up the leftovers." "Well, then, let me straighten things up a little." "No, I need to do that. I know where everything belongs."

By now, the man is totally exasperated because he is trying to help his wife, but she is rejecting all of his suggestions. He doesn't realize that what the woman really wants is for him to take her in his arms and tell her how much she is appreciated.

WHAT A WOMAN IS THINKING IS OFTEN DIFFERENT FROM WHAT SHE IS SAYING.

While she would also probably appreciate his help, she first needs emotional contact with him so that she can be emotionally stabilized. Then she will be able to tackle the other problems, and they won't seem as insurmountable. What she was *thinking* was that she could handle things if she received some love and affection from her husband. What she *expressed* was her overwhelming feelings of overload and fatigue, which her husband interpreted as a need for him to solve her problems by taking action.

A woman doesn't always tell a man what she is thinking. When she starts to become emotional, he needs to be patient and try to work through her emotions to find out what she is thinking. Sometimes, he has to dig deep to find out what is actually on her mind, because what a woman is thinking is often different from what she is saying.

This process can take patience on the part of the man, because he wants just the facts and likes to quickly arrive at the bottom line. A woman is thinking on a variety of levels, however, and it takes her longer to process all these details and arrive at a conclusion. For example, a man asks his wife, "Honey, are you still planning to serve dinner at six o'clock?" She hesitates for a moment and then says, "I still have to mash the potatoes and make the gravy." "Oh," her husband will say, "then what time will we be eating?" "Well, I also need to warm the rolls." "Okay," he says with growing impatience, "but what time are we going to eat?" "It depends on what time the roast finishes," she answers, "and Susan said she might not arrive until 6:15." "*Are we or are we not eating at six o'clock?*" he says between clenched teeth. (Pause). "No. It'll be six-thirty." "That's all I wanted to know," he says wearily as he walks away. He wanted a yes or no answer, but she was thinking on many levels and first had to work through all the many details of meal preparation and scheduling to see whether or not she could serve the meal at six o'clock.

A MAN'S HIDDEN FEELINGS

Most of the time, when a man speaks to a woman, he doesn't tell her what he's feeling. The misunderstanding this causes is what contributes to problems in relationships. For example, I've counseled many couples in which the woman doesn't understand the man's nature. "He doesn't care about me. He doesn't tell me he loves me. He's indifferent." In her experience, this explanation seems true. But all the while the man really feels deeply. Notice that I said "feels." He feels deeply for her. The problem is that he doesn't say what he is feeling; he says what he is thinking.

Note the difference: in his heart he feels great love for her, but in his mind, this love is not always translated into specific words that he can share with her. Facts and figures are what come to his mind. He can be feeling love and enjoying his wife's company, but what comes into his head, which he communicates to her, may be the latest business report or a news item. This is why a woman becomes incredulous when she shares a romantic moment with a man and the man suddenly starts talking about needing to balance his checkbook.

Do you remember the story of the woman who asked her husband, "Do you still love me?" and he replied, "I told you that the day we got married, and it still applies! I'll let you know if I ever change my mind." His response sounds horrible. He shouldn't have said that. However, what he was basically saying was that he doesn't share his feelings very easily and that it had been hard for him to express them in the first place.

Men have to start learning to communicate their feelings to women. The Word of God says that men are to treat women with consideration. *"Husbands, in the same way be considerate as you live with your wives, and treat them with respect"* (1 Peter 3:7). Men need to treat their wives with sensitivity based on a knowledge of what their wives need, so that they can continually replenish these needs. I've seen it to be true that the happier the women are, the happier the men are. As one enlightened male said, "When Jane happy, Tarzan happy."

> **"WHEN JANE HAPPY, TARZAN HAPPY."**

It can be difficult for women to understand how very hard it is for men to express their feelings. Yet it is very important for a woman not to come to any conclusions about a man's motivations until she discovers what he is feeling. There are many men who are feeling emotions that they have difficulty verbalizing. They are hurting; they feel sad and weak inside. They feel like losers. They are depressed that they haven't been promoted for ten years and that nothing is working out with their jobs. They feel as if they have failed their wives. They feel bad, but it is hard for them to come up with the words to express their feelings. A woman needs to learn to create an environment that will enable a man to tell her what he is feeling. When she works through his thinking, she will find out what he is feeling, and she will discover that what he is feeling is often very different from what he has been saying.

If women and men are not careful, they will come to conclusions about each other's motivations without knowing what the woman is really thinking or the man is really feeling. This has caused many people to think that their marriage or relationship isn't working. After a while, they say,

"Forget this," and they walk away from the relationship. Later on, they meet somebody else and get married, hoping things will be different this time. However, they encounter the same problems as in their previous relationships. They think the problem is with the other person, when the problem is often with the communication. This cycle will continue until they learn to work through and understand the differences between women and men, why each is unique, and how God has made them to beautifully complement one another.

WHAT THE WOMAN HEARS IS AN EMOTIONAL EXPERIENCE FOR HER

In addition to having different communication styles relating to what they speak about, females and males also have different styles in the way they hear what is said to them. What a woman hears is received by her as an emotional experience, while what a man hears is received by him merely as information. They have two entirely different ways of processing language that is spoken to them.

A man doesn't have an emotional experience with what he hears. This is why it is very important for the man to understand the woman. The woman receives language in an emotional way because she is designed to absorb the world around her and to personalize it. She is designed to take in everything and incubate it. Remember the example from an earlier chapter that, if you tell a woman, "You're ugly," and say the same thing to a man, you'll get a different response from each? The man will probably look at you and say, "You're ugly, too." However, the woman will never forget you as long as you live and might even consider hiring someone to assassinate you.

HE THINKS IT'S INFORMATION; SHE FEELS IT'S PERSONAL.

Before a man speaks to a woman, he needs to think about what he is about to say and how he is about to say it. Because a woman receives everything as an emotional experience, it is very important for a man to be sensitive about her feelings. He needs to consider his words rather than saying whatever comes to his mind. He may tell his wife, "That dress is getting a little tight on you." For weeks she will be quiet; she won't speak to him. Then one day her pent-up feelings will have reached a breaking point, so that she has to release them. She'll call a friend at six o'clock in the morning, crying over what her husband said to her. Her husband will hear her crying, and will come and ask her, "What's the matter, honey?" "You tell me I'm fat, then you ask me what's the matter!" "I didn't say you were fat." "Yes, you did."

What a man tells a woman will be absorbed by her entire being. If he tells her, "That rice was a little salty today," as far as he's concerned, he's giving her information. It was salty. Yet she can hear all kinds of things in that statement: he just told her she can't cook, his mother's rice was better, he's not appreciative. When she thinks about it later, she starts to wonder if he's been with somebody else who can cook better than she can. The idea grows within her: he had lunch with someone at the office, he wants to leave her, and that's why he isn't eating her food any longer! It gets very personal. Three weeks later, they're in a restaurant and the man says, "Now *this* is good rice." He is dumbfounded when she says in response, "You didn't think my rice was good three weeks ago, did you? I'm getting out of here. I'm not eating with you anymore." They have a big fight—over what? Differences in communication. He thinks it's information; she feels it's personal.

HOW A MAN HEARS LANGUAGE

On the other hand, a woman needs to realize that when she talks to a man, he hears it only as information. He runs on information because he's a logical thinker. When she wants to talk to a man, she has to learn to tell him what she thinks, not what she feels. Sometimes a woman will become upset at something that a man has done

> THE WOMAN CRIES, BUT THE MAN CANNOT "FEEL" HER TEARS.

and will start crying. Again, a woman needs to release her emotions, and she often expresses them through her tears. However, the man says, "I'm going to leave. I'll come back when you've settled down and we can talk." To a woman, he's being cold. What he's really saying is, "I'm looking for information, and I'm not receiving any. There is no reason for me to be here." So, he goes away for a while, and then comes back and asks, "Are you ready to talk now?" He doesn't understand that the woman has been trying to communicate something to him *through* her emotions.

Because his response is related to his design, a woman needs to work with the equipment the way it's made. She can sit down and say, "Honey, I have something to say to you. I did not appreciate—and it really made me feel less valued by you—when you did not open the door for me tonight in front of our friends. I know you didn't do it intentionally, but it is important for others to know that you respect me. I love you very much, and I want to be as dignified as possible to make you proud."

A man wants a woman's information; he doesn't want her tears because he doesn't know how to respond to them. This is a serious point of difference and conflict between women and men. The woman cries, but the man cannot "feel" her tears. He feels sorry that she is crying, but he wants to know what he can do to fix things. He wants information.

THE WOMAN IS INTERESTED IN THE PARTICULARS

Another point of difference between females and males is that women are generally interested in the details, in the particulars of things, while men are usually interested in what is abstract—the principles or the philosophy related to something. Similarly, when it comes to memory, women tend to remember the details, and men tend to remember the essence of the matter.

This is why, after attending a wedding, for example, a woman can talk on the phone with a friend for hours discussing all the details of the event, such as the flowers, the music, what the bride wore, and what kind of food was served at the reception. When a man is asked, "How was the wedding?" he may get a blank look on his face and then simply say, "They got married."

THE WOMAN ALWAYS REMEMBERS

A final aspect of the differences between the communication styles of women and men is that women don't usually forget things, while men generally have to be reminded over and over.

Here again, where purpose is not known, people start to become suspicious of others' motives. The woman may bring up a previous wrong she experienced, and the man will think, "What's the matter with her? I did that five years ago, and now she's bringing it up again. I told her I was sorry. I asked her for forgiveness. This happened *five years ago*. Why won't she forget it?" He is angry at her natural inclination not to forget things. Yet that is the way she is made; she is designed not to forget.

Now, a man may remember facts related to his business, but often he will not remember dates and times and events. For example, a woman may be dressing for an evening out and call to her husband, who is in another room, "You remember that we're going to your sister's birthday party tonight, don't you?" The man will have completely forgotten. He is wearing the oldest clothes he owns and holding a big bowl of popcorn, getting ready to watch the big game. She comes into the room and says, "What are you doing?" "I wanted to watch the game. Do we have to go out?" "I reminded you three times about this party! Why can't you remember anything?"

Most men don't know the reason why women remember things, and most women can't understand why men don't recall things. It has to do with their purpose and design. Men tend to think about goals and the bottom line, while women tend to remember details. These differences are complementary. However, they can be the source of serious problems in a relationship because, when you don't understand the purpose of something, you can become suspicious of it. You can begin to suspect the person you're dealing with of having ulterior motives.

LET THE PEACE OF CHRIST RULE

I would like to close this chapter with a reminder that we are all in the process of learning to be like Christ. We are learning how to become what God originally intended for us to be when He created males and females. While we're still in that learning curve, it is important for us to be patient, kind, and considerate with one another's failings as well as distinct communication styles.

Therefore, as God's chosen people, holy and dearly loved, clothe yourselves with compassion, kindness, humility, gentleness and patience. Bear with each other and forgive whatever grievances you may have against one another. Forgive as the Lord forgave you. And over all these virtues put on love, which binds them all together in perfect unity. Let

*the peace of Christ rule in your hearts, since as members of one body
you were called to peace.* (Colossians 3:12–15)

Understanding that God designed females and males with different communication styles will go a long way to helping us bear with one another in love.

> **INSTEAD OF A REACTION, GIVE A RESPONSE.**

I try not to allow others' actions to cause a reaction in me, because I am aware of people's motivations and communication styles. Instead of a reaction, I give them a response. To react is to take action against someone else before thinking. To respond is to act responsibly in your dealings with others because you understand their motivations and circumstances. A *reacting* person does what is irresponsible by becoming angry or resentful at another's behavior. But a *responding* person takes responsibility by seeking to understand the other person and by *"speaking the truth in love"* (Ephesians 4:15).

Jesus understood people thoroughly, and He also knew who He was. Understanding the nature of others—and yourself—is crucial to maintaining right relationships and not falling prey to selfishness, pride, resentment, or bitterness, which sow seeds of conflict with others.

As redeemed women and men, we are called to peace with one another. What Paul wrote about Christ bringing reconciliation between Jews and Gentiles also applies to the male-female relationship: *"For he himself is our peace, who has made the two one and has destroyed the barrier, the dividing wall of hostility"* (Ephesians 2:14).

PRINCIPLES

1. God made women and men different in the way they think, act, and respond.

2. The woman is an emotional feeler.

3. The man is a logical thinker.

4. The different communication styles of women and men are meant to be complementary.

5. A woman does not need to apologize for her emotions, because God designed her to feel.

6. When women and men understand the differences in their communication styles, they can learn how to use their differences for the betterment of them both.

7. What a woman speaks is an expression of what she feels. What a man speaks is an expression of what he thinks.

8. A woman receives what she hears as an emotional experience. A man receives what he hears as information.

9. Women are interested in the concrete details, while men are interested in abstract ideas. Similarly, when it comes to memory, women tend to remember the details and men tend to remember the essence of the matter.

10. Women don't forget, but men have to be reminded again and again.

11. Colossians 3:12–15 shows us how to bear with one another's different communication styles.

CHAPTER NINE STUDY QUESTIONS

QUESTIONS FOR REFLECTION

1. Describe a time when you had trouble communicating with your spouse or another person of the opposite sex. What difficulties in communication did you run into? What response did you both have to the situation? Did you resolve the problem? If so, how?

EXPLORING GOD'S PRINCIPLES AND PURPOSES

2. The primary difference in communication style between women and men is that a woman is generally an "_____ _____" while a man is chiefly a "_____ _____." (p. 165)

3. Describe the woman's communication style. (pp. 165–166)

4. What is the basic difference in brain structure between women and men? (p. 166)

5. What was God's purpose in creating women and men with different ways of looking at life? (pp. 166–167)

6. How does the woman's communication style help the man's perspective? (p. 167)

7. Why did God design the man to focus on the "cold hard facts" of a situation? (p. 169)

8. On the other hand, why is it important for a man to balance logic with feeling? (p. 170)

9. What a woman is _____ is often different from what she is _____. (p. 174)

10. When a woman is emotional about a circumstance or issue, what should a man do to understand what she is thinking? (pp. 173–174)

11. Why is it that a woman can share a romantic moment with a man and the man suddenly starts talking about his work or needing to balance his checkbook rather than expressing his feelings for her? (pp. 174–175)

12. What does a man need to consider before he speaks to a woman? (pp. 176–177)

13. What does a woman need to realize before she talks to a man? (pp. 177–178)

14. What is the difference between reacting to others' words or actions and responding to them? (pp. 179–180)

CONCLUSION

Women and men need to understand the strengths of each other's God-given communication styles and learn to communicate with one another according to the style the other party can receive and understand. With this knowledge—and some patience and forgiveness—females and males who are seeking God's redemptive purposes for their lives can communicate with one another effectively and happily while working together for their mutual benefit.

APPLYING GOD'S PRINCIPLES TO YOUR LIFE

THINKING IT OVER

+ Women often have been written off as foolish and inferior by men because they are expressive and show their emotions. Many males have assumed that their approach is better than the females' approach, rather than complementary to it. If you are a man, have you dismissed women's emotions and perceptions as irrational or unproductive? What have you learned about the value of a woman's gifts of communication? If you are a woman, have you realized the importance of the way you look at life for the fulfillment of God's purpose for the world?

PRAYING ABOUT IT

+ Ask God to help you understand your mate's communication style and enable you to communicate with your spouse according to the style he or she can receive and understand.

+ Colossians 3:13 says, *"Bear with each other and forgive whatever grievances you may have against one another. Forgive as the Lord forgave you."* Mutual love and respect is crucial to lasting relationships. It is important for us to be patient and kind regarding one another's failings as well as distinct communication styles. To build better relationships, forgive your spouse or other members of the opposite sex for misunderstanding your motives and perspective on life. Ask for forgiveness where you have been unkind or insensitive. Then pray that God will help you to appreciate the communication differences between women and men and to bless others through the unique gifts and perspectives He's given you.

ACTING ON GOD'S TRUTH

+ God gave females to males so that men can have balance, so that they can have the benefit of women's sensitivity and discernment. If you are a husband, make a point to talk over important decisions with your wife in order to get her input and perspective and then carefully consider what she has to say. A wife can often steer her husband away from many potential problems in his work or other endeavors.

"For he himself is our peace, who has made the two one and has destroyed the barrier, the dividing wall of hostility."
—Ephesians 2:14

TEN

UNDERSTANDING THE WOMAN'S EMOTIONAL NEEDS AND SEXUALITY

Did you know that a woman has twice as many nerve endings in her skin as a man does? Because her nerves are more numerous, they are also more susceptible to being "strained." Her skin is almost literally wired to receive a loving husband's touches of affection to soothe her frayed nerves and calm her emotions.

This physiological fact highlights the theme for this chapter: a woman's emotional and sexual needs are different from a man's by design. I want the idea of God's purpose and design to permeate your thinking about the relationship between females and males, because it is such a fundamental principle, has so many applications, and is crucial to understanding the differences between them.

Here are some of the major differences between men and women:

- Women tend to takes things to heart; men tend to take things impersonally.

- In material things, women tend to look at the goals; men want to know how to get there.

- In spiritual or intangible things, the opposite is true. Men look at the goals; women want to know how to get there.

- Women are like computers; their minds keep processing in the background until a problem is solved. Men are like filing cabinets. They take problems, put them in the file, and close the drawer.

- A woman's home is an extension of her personality; a man's job is an extension of his personality.

+ Women have a great need for security and roots; men can be nomadic.

+ Women tend to be guilt-prone; men tend to be resentful.

+ Women are constantly changing; men level off and stay the same.

+ Women tend to become involved with things more easily and more quickly; men tend to stand back and evaluate.

Considering these differences, in addition to the others we've discussed throughout this book, we shouldn't wonder why men and women have misunderstandings and conflicts in their relationships!

Remember one of our primary principles? Purpose determines design (or nature), and design determines needs. The above differences are related to the specific designs of women and men. Their designs, in turn, determine the needs of each that need to be met in order for them to be fulfilled, contented, and living in God's creation purposes.

The problem is that many people are not fully aware of their own needs, let alone the needs of others. Over the past twenty years, I have been counseling couples, and the greatest problem I have seen is that husbands and wives don't know that the needs of their spouses are different from their own.

Even when people are aware of their needs, they often live in frustration because their needs are not being met. They end up demanding that another person satisfy them or they suffer in silence, never expecting to live a completely fulfilled life.

In this chapter, I want to highlight three paramount needs of females and males that contribute to a fulfilling relationship. It is important for us to keep these needs centrally in mind as we interact with our spouses and others with whom we are in relationship. As we come to understand ourselves and others better, and how we can help to meet others' needs, our hearts and minds will be renewed and more of God's creation purposes will be restored to our lives.

Women and men must understand that fulfillment can come only when they work together to address one another's needs. In this endeavor, Jesus' great principle, *"It is more blessed to give than to receive"* (Acts 20:35), is vital. As you give, meeting the needs of others, you will be blessed, and many of your own needs will be met in turn. Giving to others by satisfying their needs—not demanding to have your own needs satisfied—will bring true fulfillment.

> A WOMAN DOESN'T JUST WANT LOVE, SHE TRULY NEEDS IT BY DESIGN.

Some of the ideas in this chapter we have discussed in other contexts, while other ideas are new. We must allow these principles to permeate our understanding so that they will become part of our lives. Please keep in mind that the needs that are listed as female needs and the needs that are listed as male needs are also the needs of both. However, in this chapter they will be discussed in the context of the *primary* needs of each. If we can learn and apply the following principles, we will go a long way to healing broken lives, promoting understanding, and developing strong relationships between women and men.

THE WOMAN NEEDS LOVE

The primary need of the female-man is love. We have learned that the woman was *designed* to receive love. This truth is so central to a woman's emotional needs that if it is the only one that men learn and apply, it will make a vast difference in women's lives—and consequently in their own.

A woman doesn't just want love, she truly needs it by design. This is why a man can give her a house and expensive gifts and she will still not feel satisfied. The man will say, "What's wrong with you? I can't do anything to please you. I'm giving you all these things, and you're still unhappy." She will answer, "It is not this mink coat or this house that I really want. I want *you*. I want you to tell me I'm important and special and unique to you, and that I am everything you've been dreaming of. I want you to tell me you love me."

You can't replace love. To love means to cherish, to care for, and to show affection. Cherishing a woman doesn't mean buying her expensive presents; it means calling her several times a day and telling her that you love her.

Caring means that you go out of your way to make sure that she has everything she needs. It means dropping everything you're doing just to make certain she is all right. Love doesn't say, "I'm busy right now. I'll talk to you later." Caring is making other people wait while you meet the needs of your wife.

Affection is the environment in which to grow a wonderful marriage. A woman's need for affection can be met with plenty of hugs and kisses; a steady flow of words, cards, and flowers; common courtesies; and meaningful gifts that show the man is thinking of her, esteems her, and values her presence in his life.

A man can also meet a woman's need for love by providing her with financial security. This will make her feel cared for and protected. In addition, when a man spends time with a woman, it makes her feel loved because she knows she comes first in his life.

Balancing financial provision and quality time with his wife often creates the greatest challenge for a man because providing for his wife usually requires that he be away from her while he is at his workplace. However, when a man spends 'many hours' overtime at his job trying to "get ahead" but neglects his wife (and family), she will not feel loved, even though they may have millions of dollars in the bank.

If a woman is single, receiving love is still her greatest need. She also needs the affirmation and companionship of men. It is the way she is designed. Fathers, uncles, brothers, and male friends can recognize a single woman's need and show brotherly love by acts of kindness, companionship, and assistance during life's difficulties.

A MAN NEEDS RESPECT

Because the female's primary need is for love, she often thinks that the male's primary need is for love, also. He needs love, but he has a need that is even greater than that.

If a female expresses love to a male, without fulfilling this other need, he might not respond in the way she expects him to. He might remain somewhat distant. For example, a woman may wonder why her husband doesn't seem satisfied in the relationship when she has been lovingly trying to help him by

> AS MUCH AS A WOMAN NEEDS TO FEEL SHE IS LOVED, A MAN NEEDS TO KNOW HE IS RESPECTED.

keeping the household running smoothly and providing for his material needs. A woman might even write her husband love notes and give him lots of affection, but notice that he still doesn't seem happy. She wonders, "What else can I do for this man?"

Yet a male feels about those things in the same way that a female feels about the male's provision of a house. He is grateful that his material and emotional needs are being taken care of, and he appreciates his wife's efforts. However, these things don't address his primary need.

As much as a woman needs to *feel* that she is loved, a man needs to *know* that he is respected. Being respected is at the core of his self-esteem, and it affects every other area of his life. *"Each one of you [husbands] also must love his wife as he loves himself, and the wife must respect her husband"* (Ephesians 5:33).

A woman can meet a man's need for admiration and respect by understanding his value and achievements more than anyone else. She needs to remind him of his capabilities and help him to maintain his self-confidence. She should be proud of her husband, not out of duty, but as an expression of sincere admiration for the man with whom she has chosen to share her life.

Paralleling the situation of the single woman, a single man needs respect as much as a married man does. He needs the respect and affirmation of women because he is designed to need it. The women in a single man's life can meet his need by recognizing his value and accomplishments as a man and by encouraging him in his talents and lifework.

A husband is to love and cherish his wife. A wife is to respect and honor her husband. In this way there will be a constant meeting of the other's primary needs.

WHAT DO I DO IN THE MEANTIME?

One of the problems a woman may face is that her husband doesn't know he's supposed to love her in the way I've just described. This is a very real problem. Even though a woman might be honoring and esteeming her husband, he might not be showing her love because he really doesn't know how. Both men and women need to understand and meet each other's needs. However, if the woman understands their needs but her spouse doesn't, it is important that she have patience. She needs to respond to her husband according to what he knows.

If I know that a person is ignorant, I can't be angry at him. Jesus is the highest model of this for us. He said, *"Father, forgive them, for they do not know what they are doing"* (Luke 23:34). The difficulty comes when you know that a person is aware of what he's supposed to be doing but still doesn't do it. In this case, some kind of reproof is necessary. Depending on the situation, a woman might appeal directly to her husband; or she might appeal to the pastor, a trusted Christian friend, or even a family member to speak to her husband for her. Yet her best appeal is to pray for her husband and allow the Lord to change him.

However, you can't reprove an ignorant person. You can reprove a person who has knowledge, but you need to overlook the faults of a person who is ignorant. This will keep bitterness from taking over your heart. Avoid blaming the other person, live responsibly before God, and make sure you carry out your own responsibilities to your spouse. Trust God to teach your partner how to meet your needs.

THE WOMAN NEEDS CONVERSATION

In addition to love, a female needs conversation. She enjoys talking with others. This sounds so simple, but it is a real need based on her nature. A woman needs to have a man talk with her. Notice that I said *with* her and not *to* her. Because males have a leadership mind-set, sometimes their conversations with their wives amount to instructions rather than a give-and-take dialogue.

The man should always make a point to converse with the woman. Costly gifts don't mean anything to a woman if the man just leaves them with her and then walks away. She'd rather have the conversation.

The man can fulfill a woman's need for intimate conversation by continually making a point to communicate with her. To truly meet her need, he should talk with her at the *feeling* level and not just the knowledge and information level. She needs him to listen to her

> A MAN SHOULD SHOW A DESIRE TO UNDERSTAND HIS WIFE, NOT TO CHANGE HER.

attitudes about the events of her day with sensitivity, interest, and concern. All of his conversations with her should convey a desire to understand her, not to change her. This means that he should not necessarily immediately try to solve her problems for her. He needs to resist the impulse to offer solutions and instead offer his full attention and understanding.

After giving her plenty of time to express her feelings, he should conduct his end of the conversation with courtesy and openness, looking her in the eyes and telling her what he really thinks and feels. He should share his plans and actions clearly and completely, because he regards himself as accountable to her, and ask for her input. This will enable her to trust him and feel secure.

Some men say, "What am I going to talk about with my wife?" They don't realize that the woman has a need to express herself and therefore has much within her that she wants to share. A man can simply say, "What's on your mind?" and she'll usually have no problem carrying the conversation. All he has to say in response is, "Uh-huh. Oh, I see." However, he has to make sure he is really listening!

A woman can create opportunities for conversing with her husband by developing an interest in his job, his activities, and his hobbies, such as sports, music, or computers. As much as the woman needs conversation, the man needs to share his interests with her. These related needs are a natural bridge of communication between them.

For example, if he's in the middle of watching a ballgame, it would not be constructive to say, "Shut that thing off; I'm tired of this." That won't create an atmosphere for conversation but will usually cause tension. Instead, she can walk into the room in which he is watching television and say, with genuine interest, "Honey, they just caught that ball, and now they're kicking it again. What are they doing that for?" The man will immediately start talking, because he likes to discuss his interests and pursuits.

Here is another illustration. If the woman goes into the room where the man is watching his favorite team compete and says, "I want to talk to you," he will probably say, "Right after they finish this play." When she comes back in a few minutes and says, "I said I want to talk to you," he will answer, "Right after the next play." This will likely continue throughout the entire game. Instead, a woman can say, "Sweetheart, I'd like to talk to you, but let's watch this game together first. I want you to tell me everything about this game." Now the woman has really succeeded, because the man is doing what he likes, but she has gotten him to talk about it, too. After the game, she will likely have his full attention in the matter about which she wanted to talk to him.

So, if women can get involved with men in their sport or any other interest they have, they can actually develop an atmosphere for conversation. Many women would truly be amazed at what would happen if they would learn to be interested in what their husbands are interested in.

THE MAN HAS A NEED FOR RECREATIONAL COMPANIONSHIP

While the female has a need for conversation, the male has a need for recreational companionship. Notice that both of these needs have to do with sharing the company of others. This is why, when the woman participates in the man's recreational interests, he will begin to converse with her. She is sharing one of his basic needs with him, and he appreciates it.

I wish I could plant in the minds of women how important a man's need for recreational companionship is. It has to do with how he is designed. Because the man was created first and has a leader-

> NOTHING BLESSES A MAN MORE THAN WHEN A WOMAN IS INVOLVED IN HIS RECREATION.

ship nature, he seems to have an inborn need to protect his "domain" or "territory" from threats from the outside world. He is a protector. This is why a man needs to feel as if he is always winning at life. (You women may have noticed this trait already.) This need translates into a desire to win over the competition in a sports event or to master a particular area of interest or expertise. It is this territorial nature that leads to his need for recreational companionship. He needs to be involved in challenging activities, and although he likes to win, he also likes to share these experiences with others.

Nothing blesses a man more than when a woman is involved in his recreation. I can't emphasize enough how important this is. As I mentioned in the last section about a woman's need for conversation, if a woman participates in whatever a man enjoys doing—playing tennis, visiting historical landmarks, playing an instrument, or designing computer programs, for example—and lets him tell her all about it, she can strengthen her relationship with him. He will feel good when she is involved with him in his recreation.

I've seen men pick up other women who participate in their recreational activity because they need the companionship. A wife may prevent this from happening if she becomes involved in her husband's interests. If a man gains a sense of accomplishment through performing music, she should become familiar with his music. Whatever he considers his form of competition or whatever he is involved in that makes him feel as if he is shaping his own environment, she should become a part of.

I've heard women say things about their husbands such as, "That old fool; he's always over at the ball field playing softball. I wish he would stop that and come home and be a husband." This attitude won't help the situation. He has a need that is being met out there on the ball field. Why would a man spend hours on something unless he has a need that is being fulfilled through it? Instead of fighting against what brings fulfillment to the man, the woman should find out why it is important to him. Then, if possible, she should participate in it so that they can experience it together, thus building understanding, companionship, and intimacy in their relationship.

THE WOMAN NEEDS AFFECTION

Third, a woman needs affection. This need is a part of who she is. A woman doesn't just want affection—she needs it!

Yet while one of her primary needs is affection, one of the male's primary needs is sex. If these two interrelated needs are not lovingly understood and balanced, they can cause some of the worst conflicts in a marriage.

What men and women need to understand is that *affection creates the environment for sexual union* in marriage, while *sex is the event*. Most men don't realize this, and so they immediately go after the event. They don't know what it means to create an environment of affection. They focus only on their need. Men need sex, but women need affection, and they need this affection to precede sexual intimacy.

These differences, again, have to do with the distinct natures of males and females. The male was designed as the source. Not only was he the source "material" for the creation of the female, but also he was given the source for creating new life through his seed or sperm. He is the provider of the seed, and therefore his natural inclination is to provide this source. This is one of the reasons why he concentrates on the event of sex.

The woman, on the other hand, is the one who gestates the new life. Her role is to provide a warm and secure environment in which the life can grow and develop. As an incubator, the woman's natural focus is on the sensory, intuitive, and emotional realms of life, and this is why she has a corresponding need for affection. She needs an environment of affection in order to feel loved and fulfilled.

The problem is that the man is not naturally affectionate. Many men simply do not understand how to give affection to their wives. How can a man give a woman what she needs when he feels he doesn't have what she needs?

The man can learn to be affectionate. He can come to know the woman's purpose and design and then meet her need for affection as it relates to her design.

THE WOMAN'S SEASONS

While a man is always sexually ready, a woman is not always ready for sexual relations. God designed her to be on a four-season cycle: summer, winter, autumn, and spring. You can always tell

> MEN ARE TO BE CONSIDERATE TO THEIR WIVES IN SEXUAL MATTERS.

when it's summer. The sun is at high noon—hot. God made her that way. Then comes autumn. Autumn is when the weather grows cooler and the woman begins acting a little more reserved. Then winter comes, and the man feels as if he's been left out in the cold. Yet winter passes and suddenly spring arrives, it gets warmer, and everything is new again. A man needs to understand about the seasons of a woman. He might be ready, but for her, it could be wintertime.

Paul wrote, "*Encourage the young men to be self-controlled*" (Titus 2:6), and, "*Teach the older men to be temperate, worthy of respect, self-controlled*" (Titus 2:2). Peter wrote, "*Husbands, in the same way be considerate as you live with your wives, and treat them with respect*" (1 Peter 3:7).

Men are to be considerate and respectful to their wives in sexual matters. They need to be aware that the woman's design is related to her purpose. She is designed to reproduce, and therefore her body has a reproductive cycle. Even though the man is the one who plants the seed, he has to plant it during the right season for the female. God designed her differently from a man because of her purpose in reproduction. The man needs to cooperate with this purpose so that both parties can be blessed.

Some men have absolutely no consideration for their wives in this matter. Lately, I've heard of many cases of marital rape. Men raping their wives is a big problem. They think that their marriage license gives them the license to force their wives. That is not being a man; it is being a beast. That is not love, it is rape, regardless of its being in the context of their legal relationship as husband and wife. This is wrong. God's design is that genuine love be present in the marriage bed, where there is sensitivity, patience, care, and affection.

Another problem is that, when a man gets his sexual needs met, he usually believes the woman's needs have also been met. This is not necessarily the case. Just because the man is satisfied doesn't mean that the woman is, because a woman's needs are different from a man's. She experiences sexual union differently from the way in which he does. The man's responsibility is to meet a woman's needs by creating an environment of affection in which she can be fulfilled. If he creates this environment, then he will often have his own sexual need fulfilled.

What is affection? Giving affection to a woman means appealing to that which makes her an emotional being. We discussed some of what a man can do to express affection for his wife in the section on a woman's need for love. Bringing her flowers, calling her every day, sending her little cards even though it's no particular "occasion," touching her, going shopping with her, and holding her hand while walking down the street are all expressions of affection. A man might think it's foolish to hold his wife's hand as they are walking through the mall, but she will think it's wonderful. The companionship they share will create an environment of affection.

Some women think, "I wish he would go shopping with me just once and push the cart in the food store." Many men would respond to this, "Me, push a grocery cart? She does the shopping." Yet the woman wants the man to say, "Let's do the shopping together. We can finish it faster that way, and then we'll have time to go for a drive." That's affection. When he goes in the kitchen and helps her cook, that's affection. When he says, "Honey, I'll cut up the onions. Let *my* eyes water for once," that's affection. "Where's my dinner?" is not affectionate.

Showing affection is expressing one's love constantly in little ways. Many men don't know how to do this because they didn't have fathers who showed affection to their mothers. Hopefully, their sons will be better at it.

Many women just want to get sex over with because they aren't being given this kind of affection. The woman may hate the experience and then walk away from it with bitterness because while the man has been fulfilled, he

> **AFFECTION IS SOMETHING THAT THE MAN HAS TO INITIATE.**

hasn't tried to fulfill her needs. Women have said to me during marriage counseling, "I feel like I'm just being used by this 'man of God.' How can he pray all the time, read the Bible constantly, and preach, and then come home and treat me like I'm a prostitute?"

May it not be so among us. A woman doesn't want a man to jump in bed and then jump right out again. He gets exactly what he wants, but she doesn't receive anything.

Paul said that women must be treated with sensitivity and affection. Ephesians 5:28 says, *"Husbands ought to love their wives as their own bodies. He who loves his wife loves himself."* A husband is to love his wife, cherish her, and care for her, like his own body. Some men keep themselves very physically fit. They go jogging, exercise, and lift weights. God is saying, "Put the same attention on your wife." Men take care of their bodies; they shower and shave. God is saying, "Take care of her the same way you take care of yourself."

Affection is something that the man has to initiate. If a man is not sure how to be affectionate, he should sit down with his wife and say, "Tell me how to be affectionate." Men need to be trained in this. I can tell you right now that there are thousands upon thousands of men who know nothing about affection. They know much about sex, but nothing about affection.

When a woman says to her husband, "Hug me," she is not saying she wants to go to bed. She is saying she wants affection. If the man holds her, and holds her long enough, he will be rewarded.

A MALE IS ALWAYS READY

Why is the male the way he is? Design determines needs. The male was designed to be a leader, a teacher, a cultivator, and a protector. Therefore, he is wired always to be ready to act. It is his nature to be ready all the time. A leader can't be ready only sometimes. If attack comes in the middle of the night, he has to be prepared. If attack comes at midday, he can't be caught off guard. If problems arise at sunset, a leader has to be a leader. Because God designed the male to be ready, he is in a state of readiness in all the various aspects of his life, including his sexuality. His sexual energy never stops. It may pause, but it never really stops.

Many women interpret this aspect of the male as being unnatural. Yet because it is his nature always to be prepared, his body has been designed in that way, as well. Therefore, it's not unnatural for a man always to be sexually ready. The man needs to realize that being ready doesn't always mean taking action.

"Encourage the young men to be self-controlled" (Titus 2:6). Self-control is a recurring theme in Paul's writings. He knew that sex can control men. When you're always ready, you must be able to exercise self-control. A man's need for sex is one of the strongest needs imaginable. It is an aspect of the makeup of a man that gives him great fulfillment. Many men don't understand this drive themselves.

Some men believe that whenever they experience sexual desire, they have to find someone with whom to release it. They even pay to try to meet this need, yet they still aren't satisfied. They don't understand that God made them ready because of the leadership purpose He's given them. Therefore, their energy should be channeled into positive leadership.

The man's readiness places the woman in a difficult situation at times. First, she may interpret the man's sexual energy as animalistic, thoughtless, and heartless. If his approach is too abrupt or too aggressive, she may tell him to leave her alone. The man then interprets her reaction as disinterest or disrespect. In this case, he may feel inclined to find interest and respect somewhere else.

On the other hand, I've known some women who pay more attention to church activities and evangelism than they do to their husbands. In a sense, they neglect their husbands' sexual needs because they claim they are too busy serving God. However, this means that their husbands are then left at home alone—and they're always ready.

Paul told us that this type of situation is a recipe for disaster. He said that whenever a husband and wife forgo sexual relations in order to serve God, they should do so only by mutual consent and only for a short period of time.

> *The husband should fulfill his marital duty to his wife, and likewise the wife to her husband. The wife's body does not belong to her alone but also to her husband. In the same way, the husband's body does not belong to him alone but also to his wife. Do not deprive each other except by mutual consent and for a time, so that you may devote yourselves to prayer. Then come together again so that Satan will not tempt you because of your lack of self-control.* (1 Corinthians 7:3–5)

This passage means that if you are going to pray and fast, spend time with the Lord, or go on a missions trip, you should get the consent of your spouse before you abstain from sexual relations. It is important for a woman to be sensitive to her husband's need for sex. When some women become Christians, they somehow think that it is not "spiritual" for them to engage in physical relations any longer. They tell their husbands, "I'm saved now, and my body is the temple of the Holy Spirit, so don't touch me." This is a foolish philosophy and a damaging witness to their husbands. Sex was part of God's original design for humanity, and it is a holy thing between a husband and a wife. The Bible says to the woman, *"The wife's body does not belong to her alone but also to her husband"* (1 Corinthians 7:4), and it says to the man, *"The husband's body does not belong to him alone but also to his wife"* (v. 4).

> **SEX IS PART OF GOD'S ORIGINAL DESIGN FOR HUMANITY AND IS A HOLY THING BETWEEN HUSBAND AND WIFE.**

The wife's body belongs both to herself and to her husband. The husband's body belongs both to himself and to his wife. These verses are not only telling us that husbands and wives are to meet one another's sexual needs, but also that one or the other partner has a say in whether or not she or he is ready to have sexual relations. The husband may say, "Honey, I'm ready," but she has the right to say, "You're always ready, but I'm not ready right now." There has to be a balance between having one's needs fulfilled and showing consideration for the other person's needs.

Some men walk around with the attitude, "If I don't have it, I'm going to die." Well, let them "die," then, because it's not true. The man is always ready, so he needs to exercise some self-control. As Peter said, a husband is to be sensitive to his wife's needs. He is to live with her with knowledge and consideration.

LEARNING AND FULFILLING ONE ANOTHER'S NEEDS

The primary areas of need, therefore, for women and men are love/respect, conversation/recreational companionship, and affection/sex. If you want to be blessed, don't focus on your needs but discover what the other person's needs are and seek to fulfill them. This will become a double blessing, because meeting the needs of the other person usually causes him or her to want to fulfill yours. Whenever you are not receiving what you need in a relationship, check to see if you are fulfilling these basic needs first.

There are people who say to me, "But I've been married for forty years. You don't know our marriage. I've tried everything to make it work." The Bible says that God's people perish, not because of sin, not because of the devil, but because of a lack of knowledge. (See Hosea 4:6.) Therefore, where there is a breakdown in communication or any other problem, there is often something more you need to learn about your partner's needs and your own creation design that can meet those needs.

Physically abusive situations are a separate issue and need to be addressed individually. If you are in such a situation, I urge you to seek the help of your pastor and trusted Christian friends. However, many situations in which couples are facing mild to severe marital difficulties are a result of their failure to understand, serve, and appreciate each other. Coming to understand their spouse's needs and seeking to fulfill them while offering unconditional love has transformed the marriages of numerous couples. If you will apply the principles in this chapter, I believe they will make a significant positive difference in your relationships.

These principles are drawn directly from God's Word. We need continual training in God's principles. It is good for us to receive instruction on how to properly fulfill the purposes for which we were created. In this way, we can have a positive impact on the people who need us to fulfill our purpose so that they can fulfill theirs. The Bible is our instruction manual that explains to us our purpose: *"All Scripture is God-breathed and is useful for teaching, rebuking, correcting and training in righteousness, so that the man of God may be thoroughly equipped for every good work"* (2 Timothy 3:16–17).

The Bible equips us to be the women and men that we were designed to be. I encourage you to be a person of the Word as you undertake to understand God's purposes and design for humanity and seek to meet the needs of those with whom you are in relationship. May you be blessed as you are a blessing to others.

PRINCIPLES

1. The needs of females and males are connected to their purposes and designs.

2. A primary need of the female is love, while a primary need of the male is respect.

3. To love means to cherish, to care for, and to show affection.

4. Even though a woman might be honoring and esteeming her husband, he might not know how to express love to her in the way she needs him to.

5. If a woman's husband is ignorant of her need for love, it is important that she be patient and trust God to reveal this need to him while avoiding bitterness.

6. A primary need of the female is conversation, while a primary need of the male is recreational companionship.

7. To truly meet his wife's need for conversation, a husband should talk with her at the *feeling* level and not just the knowledge and information level.

8. A husband should converse with his wife with courtesy and openness, telling her what he thinks and feels. He should share his plans and actions clearly and completely because he considers himself accountable to her.

9. A woman can create opportunities for conversing with her husband by developing an interest in his job, his activities, and his hobbies.

10. A primary need of the female is affection, while a primary need of the male is sex.

11. Sex was part of God's original design for humanity, and it is a holy thing between a husband and a wife.

12. Affection creates the environment for sexual union in marriage, while sex is the event.

13. A man should be sensitive to the seasons of a woman's reproductive cycle and not pressure her into having sexual relations, while a woman should be sensitive to her husband's need for sex.

CHAPTER TEN STUDY QUESTIONS

QUESTIONS FOR REFLECTION

1. Some of the major differences between men and women are listed on pages 186–187 of this chapter. In what ways have you seen these differences manifested in your own relationships or in the relationships of others? What conflicts or humorous incidents have come about as a result of them?

EXPLORING GOD'S PRINCIPLES AND PURPOSES

2. What does Dr. Munroe say is the greatest problem between husbands and wives that he has encountered in twenty years of counseling couples? (p. 187)

3. The primary need of the female is _____. (p. 188)

4. Why won't material gifts ultimately satisfy a woman? (p. 188)

5. To love means to _____, to _____ _____, and to _____ _____. (p. 188)

6. What can a husband do to create an environment of love and affection for his wife? (p. 189)

7. The male's greatest need is for _____. (p. 189)

8. How can a wife meet this need? (p. 190)

9. What should a woman do when her husband isn't meeting her needs, either out of ignorance or neglect? (pp. 190–191)

10. A second essential need of the female is _____. (p. 191)

11. In what ways can a man fulfill a woman's need for intimate conversation? (pp. 191–192)

12. A second essential need of a male is _____ _____. (p. 193)

13. How can a woman create opportunities for conversing with a man? (pp. 192–193)

14. A female's third primary need is _____, while a male's third primary need is _____. (p. 194)

15. God designed the woman to be on a four-season _____, and He designed the man to be always sexually _____. (p. 195)

16. If a man doesn't know how to be affectionate to his wife, what should he do? (p. 197)

17. A woman needs to be _____ to her husband's need for sex. (p. 199)

18. If you do not feel that your primary needs are being fulfilled, what should you do? (p. 200)

CONCLUSION

It is very important for healthy male-female relationships that we keep these primary needs of love/respect, conversation/recreational companionship, and affection/sex centrally in mind. Women and men must understand that fulfillment can come only when they work together to address one another's needs. In this endeavor, Jesus' great principle, *"It is more blessed to give than to receive"* (Acts 20:35), is vital. As you give, meeting the needs of others, you will be blessed, and many of your own needs will be met in turn. Giving to others by satisfying their needs—not demanding to have your own needs satisfied—will bring true fulfillment. As we come to understand ourselves and others better, and how we can help meet others' needs, our hearts and minds will be renewed, and more of God's creation purposes will be restored to our lives.

APPLYING GOD'S PRINCIPLES TO YOUR LIFE

THINKING IT OVER

+ Have you believed—consciously or subconsciously—that your spouse or another member of the opposite sex has the same needs as you do?

+ If you are a man, have you been showing your love for your wife through material support and gifts alone, instead of also expressing your love in a way that meets her emotional needs?

+ If you are a woman, have you been showing your love for your husband through caring for his material and emotional needs alone, instead of also expressing your respect for him?

PRAYING ABOUT IT

+ If your spouse isn't meeting your needs, either out of ignorance or neglect, ask God to give you patience in the situation, follow the guidelines in this chapter, pray for him or her, and allow God to bring about the change.

+ Ask God for help in better meeting the needs of your spouse or another family member according to his or her gender and individual makeup.

ACTING ON GOD'S TRUTH

+ If you have a single relative or friend, think of ways in which you might help meet her or his primary needs of love or respect, and write down your ideas below. Make a point to encourage that person this week.

+ Think of ways you can help meet your spouse's three essential needs of love/respect, conversation/recreational companionship, and affection/ sex (you may want to review sections in the book that relate to these needs).

> *"It is more blessed to give than to receive."*
> —Acts 20:35

ELEVEN

SHOULD WOMEN BE IN LEADERSHIP?

I had crossed the line. I was free; but there was no one
to welcome me to the land of freedom.
I was a stranger in a strange land.
—Harriet Tubman

What we have discussed so far about God's purpose and design for females prepares us to ask one of today's most controversial questions: Should women be in leadership? For those of faith, this question usually has a specific focus: Should a woman be in a position of leadership in the church? The Word of God gives us the answers to both of these questions.

Before coming to conclusions about any issue, it is important to consider what the Word of God as a whole has to say about it. It is too easy to take one verse and build an entire doctrine upon it. This often has been the case historically as the church has looked at the question of women and leadership.

Consequently, we will explore this topic using the approach we have used throughout this book. We will look at God's purpose for the female and how it relates to leadership. To do this, we will look at examples from both the Old and New Testaments that shed light on this very important issue, so that we may have a clearer understanding of God's intent for us. At the same time, the subject of women and leadership is a very broad one and could be the theme of an entire book. Therefore we will look at the primary principles of women in leadership based on God's Word.

"I SENT YOU THREE LEADERS"

In the book of Micah, God made a remarkable statement that many people overlook and most men do not want to read.

If most males were asked, "Was Moses a great leader?" their answer would be, emphatically, yes. I believe that Moses is probably the greatest

GOD SENT A WOMAN TO LEAD.

leader in the Old Testament record, the man God chose to bring His people out of slavery in Egypt. Moses was obviously a great minister of administration. He learned much of this from his father-in-law, Jethro, who taught him to delegate rather than to take too great a load of responsibility on himself. Moses was a man of tremendous strength and character, although he was also a man of weakness. Yet God balances weaknesses with the power of His anointing. During the time of the Exodus and for forty years in the desert, Moses was an extraordinarily effective and inspiring leader.

However, I want you to read a statement God made in Micah 6:4. Women should take this verse to heart and remember it for the rest of their lives. God said, "*I brought you up from the land of Egypt, I redeemed you from the house of bondage; and I sent before you Moses, Aaron, and Miriam*" (NKJV).

God was saying, "I sent you three leaders."

We always talk about Moses, the representative and administrative leader. We also talk about Aaron, the high priest and spiritual leader. But God mentioned another leader that many men are uncomfortable reading about. He said, "I also sent Miriam to lead you."

God *sent* a woman to lead. This fact contradicts many of the attitudes that men have had for years about women in leadership. When God purposefully appointed Miriam to be a leader to His people, He endorsed the idea that it is valid for a woman to be in leadership. It is noteworthy that God did not send Miriam to lead because no men were available at the time. He sent her to lead *alongside* the men. He put her in a team of leaders. Since God acknowledged Miriam in the same list or category with Moses, we don't have to question whether God intended women to be leaders. "*I sent before you Moses, Aaron, and Miriam.*"

The Sinai leadership team included a director, a priest, and a woman. The director was Moses, the executive leader, and the priest was Aaron, the spiritual leader. Yet right in the middle of the executive leader and the spiritual leader, a woman was needed in order to bring balance to both of them. We will see the nature of her primary leadership role as we progress through this chapter.

Miriam's influential role as a leader over Israel looks back to God's purposes for the woman that He established when He created humanity, and ahead to Christ's redemptive purposes for the woman in salvation. God intended women to be leaders from the creation of the world, and He confirmed His continued commitment to this intention through the ministry of His Son, Jesus Christ. This is the basis on which we will explore the woman's role in leadership.

Throughout this book, we have seen the following:

+ Women and men (as man) are spiritually equal before God and equally as important to Him.

+ Women and men (as man) were given the dominion mandate.

+ Males and females (man's "houses") have distinct purposes and designs.

+ The complementary roles and abilities of males and females bring balance, strength, and help to each another as they fulfill God's purposes.

In light of these principles, the question people have been asking, "Should women be in leadership?" becomes an entirely different question. Instead of asking *if* women should be in leadership, we should be asking *how* they are to exercise their leadership, given their purpose and design.

What does the woman's purpose and design say about her leadership role?

REDISCOVERING THE LEADERSHIP PURPOSE OF WOMEN

First, let us consider once again that the dominion mandate was given to man, not just to the male. Therefore, it is God's purpose that the woman, as well as the man, be fruitful and multiply, and replenish, subdue, and have dominion over the earth. (See Genesis 1:28.) To have dominion means to govern, to rule, to subdue, to control, to manage, to lead, or to administrate. It is a powerful word. Both women and men were given the same assignment of dominion leadership. God

> ANYTHING GOD SAID ABOUT THE MALE-FEMALE RELATIONSHIP AFTER GENESIS 2 IS A REPAIR PROGRAM.

loves leadership and had it in mind when He created the earth. This is why He wanted the world to be cultivated and not just to remain wilderness. He loves order. When God told man to have dominion, He was telling man who he is. Man (male and female) is a leader who is to cultivate the earth.

There is no incidence of subjection, submission, or oppression of women in the first and second chapters of Genesis. In God's perfect will, there is no such arrangement. The woman and the man were both equal, blessed, subduing, ruling, and having dominion, and God said, "This is very good." Any other arrangement than this was the result of the Fall. This means that anything that God said about the male-female relationship after Genesis 2 is a repair program.

Second, recall that the purpose of something determines its design—its nature, potential, and abilities. Therefore, since God's purpose for man was leadership, He designed the man and the woman with the built-in potential and ability to be leaders.

Therefore, the leadership spirit is in every male and female. However, the way in which they *execute* dominion is different based on their distinct designs.

THE INFLUENCE-POWER OF THE WOMAN

Both the man and the woman were created to lead, but their leadership functions are determined by their specific dominion assignments. God designed the woman not only for relationship with Himself, but also to help fulfill His purposes in His great plan for humanity. Therefore, women are designed by God to execute an assignment that can only be fulfilled by women.

POSITION-POWER AND INFLUENCE-POWER

God designed the male to be a leader by position and the female to be a leader by influence. The man has *position-power,* and the woman has *influence-power.* There is a difference between these two forms of leadership.

A man receives his leadership by his position, in that he was created first, and by his being the source of the woman, for whom he is responsible.

His position has to do with his purpose in creation. The man became the head of his family by virtue of the fact that he was made first.

When God designed the female, He obviously had influence in mind. A woman is a receiver. God designed her to receive from the male and to incubate what she receives so that it can grow and develop. A woman is built to influence. Her wombs—whether physical, emotional, mental, or spiritual—have a tremendous influence on what they receive by providing a nurturing and transforming environment. There is much truth in the saying, "The hand that rocks the cradle rules the world."

Position-power and influence-power are not mutually exclusive; they are meant to be exercised together in dominion. Let me give you an example of this.

We have seen that the male is the initiator of new human life. He carries the seed of life, the sperm. This is why the male carries, as it were, the seed of the nations. In the Bible, whenever God wanted to create a new nation, He called on a man to initiate it. Yet while the man is the father of the nations, he cannot create these nations without the participation of the woman. A sperm is no good to a man without a woman, just as a seed is no good without soil.

God said to Abraham, *"Your name will be Abraham, for I have made you a father of many nations. I will make you very fruitful; I will make nations of you, and kings will come from you"* (Genesis 17:5–6). Yet no matter how much of an anointing Abraham had in order to become the *"father of many nations,"* he still needed Sarah to help him fulfill his calling.

Power and influence are equal, but different. A woman and a man are equal in leadership. The difference is in their leadership functions.

There are two important aspects of position-power. First, position-power generally comes with a title, such as king, governor, doctor, or pastor.

ABRAHAM NEEDED SARAH TO HELP HIM FULFILL HIS CALLING.

Second, position-power is usually executed through commands, whether verbal or written. It is the authority that goes with the position—and underlies the commands—that is the nature of the man's power.

Influence-power manifests itself in a very different way. First, a woman may have a title, but she doesn't need a title in order to lead. She leads by influence. This is why women usually run the households. Men call themselves "the head of the house," but the women run the homes. Second, a woman doesn't need to talk in order to run things. She leads just by her influence. My father used to run our household with his mouth. He would say, "Clean the kitchen"; "Take the garbage out"; "Take your feet off that chair." However, my mother would just *look* at me, and my feet would be down off that chair. The woman doesn't need to say a word; she just looks, and people respond. This is a powerful influence. Some men assume that because many women are quiet or don't bark out orders, they are weak. They do not understand influence-power.

THE DANGERS OF INFLUENCE-POWER

Influence-power may be more subtle and quiet than position-power, but it has a potent effect. Satan understood this influence. The fall of man resulted from the serpent's interference with influence leadership.

> SATAN WENT TO THE INFLUENCE-POWER AND USED IT TO DESTROY THE POSITION-POWER.

The devil is clever; when he wanted to destroy humanity, he went to the woman instead of the man. He was after the man, because the man is the foundation, but he couldn't get to the man because position-power can usually stand firm as long as its position is genuine. You can't destroy position-power directly; you have to destroy it through influence. Therefore, Satan went to the influence-power to get at the position-power. He hasn't changed his tactic since, because it worked so well.

The devil went to Eve and basically said, "I have a proposition for you. If you really want to be like God, pick the fruit and eat it." The Bible says that Eve looked at the fruit and saw that it was good for food and that it was beautiful. She picked it and ate it. Nothing bad appeared to happen to her, so she took it to her husband and influenced him to eat it. Satan went to the influence-power and used it to destroy the position-power.

Yet God is *all-powerful*, and He was not defeated by the devil's success. He immediately put a plan in motion that not only would restore humanity but also would defeat Satan. However, His plan meant that a new arrangement would need to be made in the relationship between females and males until His redemptive purposes could be fulfilled.

The power of a woman's influence may be seen in God's original design for her and in His response to her after the fall of man:

1. In creation, God gave the woman the assignment of rulership. This shows the respect He has for her.

2. God promised the devil that his destruction would come through the woman. He identified the woman as the instrument through which man would be redeemed.

3. The woman's influence-power, in its fallen state, is so potentially destructive that God felt He needed to put her under regulation for her own protection and the protection of others. God gave the male the assignment of regulating the influence-power of the woman until the fullness of time when He would send His Son, born of a woman, to complete the process of redeeming her place of partnership with the man.

A woman was not originally created by God to be regulated by a man. This is not God's plan for the woman. Humanity's disobedience to God is what altered her situation—but this alteration was only temporary. Because God knew the influence potential with which He had created the woman, He considered her to be more dangerous than the man in her fallen state. This is why God put her under regulation.

When God told the woman of this regulation, He was saying, in effect, "You are so powerful that I can't trust you by yourself any longer." His action with the woman is parallel to His action of banishing Adam and Eve from the Garden to prevent them from eating of the Tree of Life and thereby being doomed to live forever in their corrupt state without any opportunity for redemption. He did it for her protection.

God said to the woman in Genesis 3:16, "*I will greatly increase your pains in childbearing; with pain you will give birth to children. Your desire will be for your husband, and he will rule over you.*" The word "*rule*" means to "regulate" rather than to "boss." Now, when it came to the man, God seemed to be saying, "As for you, Adam, your position-power is not as dangerous as the woman's influence-power, so you won't need much regulation. I'm going to let thorns and thistles rule you. I'm going to let the snags and difficulties of life that you will encounter rule over you. However, the woman will need plenty of leadership."

This is why, when you meet a woman who does not have the Holy Spirit indwelling her, you are encountering a dangerous package of influence that has the potential to bring destruction without inhibition. The woman doesn't need regulation because she is the weaker vessel but because she is potentially the more dangerous one.

> THE WOMAN NEEDS REGULATION BECAUSE SHE IS POTENTIALLY MORE DANGEROUS.

What do I mean by dangerous? When a man is in charge, everybody knows it, because he announces it. "I'm here. I'm the boss." Position-power announces itself. Influence power just comes in and controls things. By the time you realize its presence, it has already taken over. Some of you who have been divorced know what I am talking about. An outside manipulative woman has come into your life and ruined your marriage. When a wife says to a husband who has been unfaithful, "How could you have done that!" he often says, "I don't know." He was waylaid by the power of influence.

A woman is more dangerous because hers is a silent power. You don't even see when she is working. It is not necessarily presidents and prime ministers who are truly running our countries. Power is not only in the state house and the White House. It is in the bedroom. A woman doesn't have to make a public policy speech. All she has to say is, "I don't think you should do that, honey," and it becomes policy. Hers is a powerful influence.

Influence-power is a tremendous gift from God that was intended to be used by women for good—for the good of themselves, their families, their communities, their nations, the world, and the kingdom of God. Yet women have to realize its potential for evil as well as for good. Even redeemed women have to be careful to discipline their influence-power. Consider these examples of corrupted influence:

+ Adam sacrificed his relationship with God when he chose Eve's influence over what God had told him. Although he was fully responsible for his action, this influence contributed to his temptation to rebel against God, which affected the future of humanity.

+ Abraham, who was called God's friend and was given the promise of a blessed son and heir by God, was influenced by his wife, Sarah, to take matters into his own hands and try to force the fulfillment of the promise through human means. When Sarah spoke, her voice became more influential to Abraham than God's, even though he had had a personal visitation from the Lord. Today, we are still seeing the consequences of this influence in the never-ending conflicts between the Arabs and the Jews.

+ Samson, whose unusual anointing enabled him to kill a thousand Philistines with the jawbone of a donkey and do other feats of strength, was influenced by Delilah to reveal the source of his strength. Then he was betrayed by her, resulting in his capture and eventual death.

The leadership of a woman is so powerful that God says it needs regulation if it isn't under the control of the Holy Spirit.

GOD WANTS TO RESTORE WOMEN TO THEIR FULL LEADERSHIP ROLE

We need to remember that, even though the woman's influence-power has the potential to harm, it was God who originally gave her this leadership gift when He created her. The *influence* is not the result of the Fall; the *corruption* of the influence is. It is God's desire that the woman be restored to her full leadership role and use this influence for His good purposes. God indicated that this was His plan even at the time of the Fall. All of the declarations that God gave Eve and Adam in Genesis 3 are God's response to the Fall. He said that, in the end, He was going to restore what He had established in the beginning. How? Through the redemption of Jesus Christ and the coming of the Holy Spirit.

When the Holy Spirit comes back into a woman's life, God's plan for her reverts to what it was originally. This is why Peter said, "*Husbands, in the same way be considerate as you live with your wives, and treat them with respect as…heirs with you of the gracious gift of life*" (1 Peter 3:7, emphasis added).

Women are joint and equal heirs of salvation with men. This means that, when a woman receives salvation in Jesus Christ, she becomes equal in rulership again. At the time of the Fall, God cursed the devil and promised that He would deal with him decisively at a later time. The seed of the woman would come and crush his head and take away his power. Let us look more closely at how God accomplished His plan of restoration for the woman (and the man) through Christ.

CHRIST RESTORED THE WOMAN TO PARTNERSHIP

> **THE BIBLE IS AN ACCOUNT OF GOD'S RESTORATION PROGRAM.**

Jesus Christ restored humanity to God's purpose and plan. I define the plan of God very simply. Genesis 1–2 is a depiction of God's perfect program for the spirit-man and his manifestation as male and female. Chapter 3 reveals how and why this program fell apart. Genesis 3 to Revelation 21, the last chapter of the Bible, explains what God has done and is still doing to restore humanity to His original program (and even beyond that). The Bible is an account of God's restoration program, which He effected through various covenants with His people.

Christ's life, death, and resurrection accomplished the redemption of man. The sacrifice of the perfect Man made atonement for the sins of fallen man and restored humanity to the fellowship with God it had enjoyed in the Garden of Eden. This means that the curse of sin is removed from people's lives when they receive Christ's redemptive work and are born again. Christ's own Spirit comes to dwell within them, they are restored to God's purposes, and they are able to love and serve God again.

Under the redemptive work of Christ, the woman is not only restored to fellowship with God but is restored to the position of partner with her male counterpart. Therefore, she is no longer to be dominated or ruled by the male, because, if she were, it would mean that the redemptive work of Christ had not been successful.

The woman was created by God to be a helper, not a slave. There is a big difference between the two. The Bible refers to the Holy Spirit as a Helper. (See John 15:26; 16:7 NKJV.) Jesus said that the Holy Spirit not only would help us, but also would lead us. *"He will guide you into all truth"* (John 16:13). The Holy Spirit is the Paraclete, meaning the One who can help as well as be a Comforter, Counselor, and Guide.

Being a helper does not mean being inferior. A helper can be a guide and a teacher. Therefore, although the male is always the responsible head in God's design, he is not the "boss." He is not the owner of the woman.

Remember that when God addresses the human race, He never addresses us as male and female; He addresses us as "man." He deals with the spirit-man within both male and female. In order to function on earth as man, however, males and females each exercise an aspect of leadership that was given to man, the spirit.

While the man is ultimately the responsible head, the woman is a coleader. A good illustration of this is the relationship between Jesus and His church. Jesus is called the Head, and the church is called the body. (See Colossians 1:18.) They work in unison with one another. Christ's relationship to the church is the perfect model for us of the male-female relationship and God's purposes for the woman in her dominion leadership role.

CHRIST'S INFLUENTIAL BRIDE

Christ's sacrificial work on the cross redeemed the power of influence in a beautiful example of God's love and purposes. When it was time for Jesus to die on the cross, He knew He was about to begin a journey that would involve something along these lines: "I have to return to My Father, but I want to influence the world for My kingdom. I am the King and I am the Word; therefore, I exercise position-power. To influence the world, I need a wife, a partner, who has influence-power."

The experience of the Second Adam is parallel with the experience of the first. For example, Jesus had to be born a male because the male is the source; moreover, Christ had to be a male because He came to fulfill what Adam had failed to do. To accomplish this, He experienced something very close to what Adam experienced when God created the woman. He who is the Second Adam went to sleep (in His death on the cross) so that God could take out of Him a woman named *ekklesia*, the church.

CHRIST LEFT THE EARTH IN THE HANDS OF A WOMAN, THE CHURCH.

When Christ's side was pierced by the spear, blood and water poured out; symbolically, the church was born of blood and water—the blood of Christ and the water of the Word. Therefore, the church was brought forth from Christ's side as the woman was brought forth from the side of the man.

The church is described in the Bible as a "she," a bride, a woman. It is given a feminine designation. As Eve was presented to Adam in perfection, Christ says that He will present to Himself *"a radiant church...holy and blameless"* (Ephesians 5:27). Jesus told His bride, "I love you." Then He said to men, "Husbands, love your wives as I love My wife." How does Christ show love to the church? He cleanses her with the washing of the water by the Word; He takes away every spot, wrinkle, and blemish (see verses 25–28), just as Adam was supposed to have done for Eve.

Adam's job was to protect Eve and to make sure that she was kept continually cleansed by communicating God's Word to her. Adam's failure was that he, in a sense, abandoned Eve, and that is why she was vulnerable to Satan's enticements. Then, when Eve went to Adam after having disobeyed God's Word, instead of correcting her, he joined with her in disobedience.

Jesus, however, is the perfect Man. He told His wife, *"Never will I leave you; never will I forsake you"* (Hebrews 13:5). This is what makes the difference. Satan cannot overcome the church, because Christ will never leave her. He's maintaining His perfect vigil over her. He is the Perfect Adam.

Before God created Eve, He first declared that she was to help Adam in fulfillment of the dominion assignment; she would be his helper. The church fulfills exactly the same role for Christ. Being a member of the body of Christ not only means receiving salvation but also helping the Lord in His purpose of winning the world to Himself. This is why He gave the church the responsibility of going into the world as a witness for Him. It is His plan to draw the world to Himself in salvation, and it is the church's role to help Him to do it.

Jesus said to His woman, "I am going to leave the entire world in your care because I need someone who can *influence* the world for Me." Therefore, Christ left the earth in the hands of a woman, the church. All Christian women and men are part of this woman.

The church helps Jesus to accomplish His redemptive assignment. He sees her as a perfect leader, and He shows this by the fact that He has entrusted the Word of God to her. Now, the implication of this is that the female is a trusted leader, just as the male is. The church is not the servant of Jesus, just as the female is not the servant of the male, but his partner. *"I no longer call you servants, because a servant does not know his master's business. Instead, I have called you friends, for everything that I learned from my Father I have made known to you"* (John 15:15).

In Christ, God's purposes have been restored. Jesus told the church, "You will be seated *with* Me in heavenly places." (See Ephesians 2:6.) He did not say, "You will be seated *below* Me." Since Christ is the King, the church is His queen. We need to see God's intent for the female in this portrayal of Christ and the church. She is not meant to sit below the man, but to be his partner in leadership, in dominion.

This principle is extremely important: when men treat women as inferior, lesser, or weak beings, when they oppress or suppress them, they are damaging themselves; they are undermining their own purpose and potential. Both the male-man and the female-man are made in God's image. Any oppression of that image is an oppression of oneself: *"He who loves his wife loves himself"* (Ephesians 5:28).

GOD'S PLAN HAS ALREADY BEEN RESTORED

What we need to fully realize is that God's plan for the woman in leadership has *already* been restored. It is not just for a future time in heaven. However, now we need to have our minds renewed in this truth so that we may understand

> GOD'S PLAN FOR THE WOMAN IN LEADERSHIP HAS ALREADY BEEN RESTORED.

and advance God's redeemed purposes for the woman. This is where the challenge currently lies in the world and especially in the church. Most churches are still struggling with the issue of women in leadership or how to translate a woman's influence-power into practice in the church.

WHAT ABOUT PAUL'S WRITINGS?

In the minds of many people in the church, the teachings of Paul regarding women in leadership either outright forbid her to participate in a leadership role or are contradictory, at best. I believe that his writings are very clear if we understand that he wrote them in the context of God's purpose and design for man (the spirit), and in the context of practical instruction for males and females who are trying to deal with the negative effects of the Fall within their own cultural environments. I believe that Paul wrote from both of these contexts.

In other words, when Paul wrote, *"There is neither Jew nor Greek, slave nor free, male nor female, for you are all one in Christ Jesus"* (Galatians 3:28), he was talking about the spirit-man, whom Christ redeemed. Therefore, in the body of Christ, in the Spirit, you're dealing with *man*, where there is no difference in gender. In other letters, Paul was addressing problems people were dealing with in places like Corinth or Ephesus, where people's cultural heritage was making it difficult for them to adjust to their new Christian faith. For example, he told the Corinthians, *"Women should remain silent in the churches. They are not allowed to speak, but must be in submission, as the Law says"* (1 Corinthians 14:34).

This passage has been terribly misunderstood and has been used as a general rule in order to keep women down, to subjugate and oppress them. Many people don't realize that, in the same letter, Paul gave instructions to women who pray or prophesy in the church. (See 1 Corinthians 11:5.) Obviously, they needed to speak in order to do that. Therefore, I believe that Paul's instructions to the Corinthians had to do with keeping order in the churches when the people's carnality or cultural background was creating confusion and discord. God is a God of order. Based on Paul's other writings and on Scriptures and biblical principles from both the Old and New Testaments, these few instructions of Paul's should not be considered the final or only word on the matter.

Today, however, because of Paul's desire to bring order to these new congregations, we have people saying that women are to be silent in the churches, wear hats, and basically be seen and not heard. They claim a woman cannot lead or preach. We have become so focused on what amounts to legalism that we are missing God's revelation of what the woman is: she is the spirit-man within the female.

Let us ask ourselves,

+ What is more important, culture or Christ?

+ What is a more valid example of God's purposes, a Spirit-filled woman or a carnal woman?

✦ Did Jesus ever command a woman to be silent?

✦ Did Jesus ever stop a woman from preaching?

As a matter of fact, the woman at the well went preaching after Jesus set her free, and then she became an evangelist.

Sometimes we make Paul's sayings more important than Jesus' own revelation of God's purposes. *Please do not misunderstand what I am saying. It is all God's Word.* Yet Paul in these statements was dealing with specific cultural issues; Christ was dealing with principles. Culture should not be confused with principles. Jesus elevated, promoted, and restored women to their original dignity. Moreover, Paul himself affirmed the woman's equality with man in Christ.

Even before Jesus died on the cross, He affirmed women in His earthly ministry in a way that was revolutionary to fallen man, but was right in line with God's purposes for man in creation. This was a striking illustration of His respect for women and their value to Him as their Creator and Redeemer.

As I wrote earlier, if you as a male have problems with a female preacher, I encourage you to close your eyes and listen to the spirit-man speaking. This approach has helped many men. Listen to what's being said. If the female house is the problem, then ignore the house and listen to the resident, the spirit-man within, because God speaks through the spirit-man. It is the Spirit that gives life. (See 2 Corinthians 3:6.)

Therefore, it is not only the male, but also the female, who can be a leader. Moreover, their leadership styles do not cancel each other out; it is the *combination* of position-power and influence-power that enables man to exercise dominion over the world and which will bring the kingdom of God on earth. The devil is in trouble when the two types of power come together in unity of purpose.

STRANGERS IN A STRANGE LAND

Trapped in every follower is an undiscovered leader, and there are many undiscovered leaders in the women of our churches. Yet women are very productive leaders. The saying is true: If you want something done, give it to a woman. Her influence-power is

TRAPPED IN EVERY FOLLOWER IS AN UNDISCOVERED LEADER.

highly effective. Even when she is in a role that has traditionally been a position-power role, she brings her influence, her instincts, and her other special gifts to this role. That is why, for example, woman make such good negotiators in government and business.

There are churches filled with women, but men don't allow them to hold responsible positions. I don't understand this. Woman are leaders; they influence positive growth and change. Men in the church will often say they will do something, and then they won't show up. Women don't say anything, but they do show up, and they influence others to come, also.

Abolitionist Harriet Tubman said that when she crossed the line to freedom, "I was free; but there was no one to welcome me to the land of freedom. I was a stranger in a strange land." Many women feel the same way about their leadership abilities. They have been set free by Christ, restored to their place of partnership, but there is no one to welcome them into this land of freedom and service for God. They feel like strangers in a strange land, even though they are supposed to be in the Promised Land of the church.

Galatians 5:1 says, "It is for freedom that Christ has set us free. Stand firm, then, and do not let yourselves be burdened again by a yoke of slavery."

It is time men welcomed women to the land of freedom.

PRINCIPLES

1. God endorsed women in leadership when He purposefully sent a woman (Miriam) to be a leader to His people.

2. Instead of asking *if* women should be in leadership, we should be asking *how* they are to exercise it, given their purpose and design.

3. The spirit-man in every male and female is a leader.

4. The execution of dominion is different for males and females based on their purpose and design. The male exercises position-power and the female exercises influence-power.

5. Power and influence are equal, but different. A woman and a man are equal in leadership. The difference is in their leadership functions.

6. Influence-power may be more subtle than position-power, but it has a potent effect.

7. When a woman is not under the influence of the Holy Spirit, her influence can become dangerous.

8. Through redemption, Christ restored the woman to full partnership with the man.

9. Paul's writings on women reflect two contexts: a woman's equality with a man based on their redemption in Christ and a cultural context.

10. Even before Jesus died on the cross, He affirmed women in His earthly ministry in a way that was revolutionary to fallen man, but was right in line with God's purposes for humanity in creation.

CHAPTER ELEVEN STUDY QUESTIONS

QUESTIONS FOR REFLECTION

1. Do women have leadership roles in your church? If so, what types of leadership positions? Do you think women should be in leadership? Why or why not?

2. Are some leadership roles acceptable for women and others not? Why?

EXPLORING GOD'S PRINCIPLES AND PURPOSES

3. What statement did God make in Micah 6:4 that is often overlooked today? (p. 208)

4. What idea did God endorse through this statement? (p. 208)

5. There is a prevalent view that God puts women in leadership positions only when there are no men to lead or the men have forfeited their leadership. How does this idea compare with Miriam's experience? (p. 208)

6. What biblical principles have we learned about God's purposes for women and men that show God intended women to be leaders from the creation of the world? (p. 209)

7. When God told man (male and female) to have dominion, what was He telling them about who they are? (p. 210)

8. The man's form of leadership is called _____-_____, and the woman's form of leadership is called _____-_____. (p. 210)

9. Are these two forms of leadership equal? Why or why not? (p. 211)

10. How does the woman's influence-power manifest itself? (p. 212)

11. When the devil wanted to destroy humanity, why did he go to the woman instead of the man? (p. 212)

12. In Genesis 3:16, the word "*rule*" means to regulate rather than to "_____." (p. 213)

13. In what ways does influence-power have the potential to be harmful? (p. 214)

14. How can a woman make sure she uses her leadership influence for good? (p. 215)

15. The woman was created by God to be a helper, not a slave. What person of the Trinity models her leadership role? What aspects of influence does He exhibit? (pp. 216–217)

16. Which of Paul's teachings has been used by many men in the church as a general rule to keep women from speaking in the church or having a leadership role in it? (p. 220)

17. In light of the above question, what other instructions did Paul give in the same book of the Bible that help clarify his perspective on women speaking in the church? (p. 220)

18. What criteria should we use to draw conclusions about God's attitude toward women in leadership? (pp. 220–221)

CONCLUSION

It is not only the male, but also the female, who can be a leader. The leadership styles of men and women do not cancel each other out. It is the combination of position-power and influence-power that enables mankind to exercise dominion over the world and help bring the kingdom of God on earth.

Most churches are filled with women, but the men often don't allow them to hold positions of responsibility. This means there are many undiscovered leaders in our churches. Women have been set free by Christ and restored to their place of partnership with men. It is time men welcomed them and encouraged them to use the God-given leadership gifts and abilities that only they can fulfill.

APPLYING GOD'S PRINCIPLES TO YOUR LIFE

THINKING IT OVER

+ In the past, what criteria have you used to decide what a woman's role in the church should be? How has your thinking changed/stayed the same as a result of this study?

+ If you are a woman, have you accepted the leadership role God has given you?

+ If you are a man, have you accepted the leadership role God has given women?

PRAYING ABOUT IT

+ Ask God to guide you into the roles (whether in your church, job, or community) that He desires for you. Then, be open to His plans, even if they are different from what you have previously expected.

ACTING ON GOD'S TRUTH

+ If you are a woman, think about whether you are using your influence-power for positive or negative purposes. Yield your influence-power to the control of the Holy Spirit. Then write down three ways in which you can use your influence for good in your family, your community, and your church.

+ If you are a man, consider the fact that it was Adam's job to protect Eve and to make sure that she was kept spiritually cleansed by communicating God's Word to her. Adam's failure was that he, in a sense, abandoned Eve by neglecting to protect her in this way, and that is why she was vulnerable to the devil's enticements. Are you protecting and building up your wife, daughter, or another female under your care through prayer and the Word of God? If not, how will you begin to do so today?

"There is neither Jew nor Greek, slave nor free, male nor female, for you are all one in Christ Jesus."
—Galatians 3:28

CONCLUSION: THE PROVERBS 31 WOMAN

No book about the purpose and power of women would be complete without discussing the woman who is considered the epitome of both womanhood and power: the woman of Proverbs 31.

Some women don't even like to read this chapter of the Bible because they are overwhelmed by all the things this woman is supposed to be able to do. "Well, if I had a staff of servants like she had, I could do all those things, too!" they exclaim. Yet when we consider our exploration of God's purposes for the woman from creation to redemption, and when we think about how the woman has been set free to fulfill His purposes, Proverbs 31 gives us tremendous perspective on what a woman is meant to be. Let us not become overwhelmed when reading about what this woman *does* and miss out on the central message of who she *is*.

One of the themes that Proverbs 31 is trying to communicate is this: The woman is a doer. She is a multitasker. She is responsible for taking care of her husband, children, home, job, talents, church commitments, charitable work, and sometimes elderly parents. She is a helper and she is a leader. She receives seed into her physical, emotional, psychological, and spiritual wombs, incubates it, and then uses it to build and transform the world around her.

However, while she is fulfilling all of these vital purposes in the home and in the world, she must always remember that a *woman's first place is in God*. Proverbs 31 reminds the woman, "Don't neglect your relationship with God, and don't forget to develop His character in your inner being as you go about your extremely busy life."

It is much too easy to begin to overlook God when you are taking care of so many other people and responsibilities. This takes us full circle to what we learned about the woman at the beginning of this book. The woman was created to be loved by God and to have fellowship with Him as a spirit-being made in His image. She was meant to reflect His character and likeness, to represent His true nature. God created the woman to have His moral characteristics within her inner being. She is not only

> **A WOMAN WANTS TO FEEL THAT SHE IS VALUED FOR THE CONTRIBUTIONS SHE IS MAKING TO HER FAMILY AND COMMUNITY.**

to resemble Him as a spirit, but also in these qualities. She was designed to act and function as God does, in love and grace. Therefore, Proverbs 31 is saying, "While you are doing what God has called and gifted you to do, don't forget the importance of His character in your life":

> *A wife of noble character who can find? She is worth far more than rubies.* (v. 10)

> *Charm is deceptive, and beauty is fleeting; but a woman who fears the* LORD *is to be praised.* (v. 30)

Women need to realize that their relationship with the Lord and the development of His character in their lives is an essential foundation that will strengthen and sustain them in all their activities and accomplishments. With continual refreshing from the Lord, they can purposefully engage in their many responsibilities and fulfill the exciting purposes God has for them.

In some ways, a woman may derive her self-esteem from her activities almost as much as a man derives his self-image from his work. She wants to feel that she is *valued* for the contribution she is making to her family and her community. Yet because she is an emotional feeler, she places this need in the context of her relationships and emotions, and so it is not as easily recognized for what it is.

Christ has freed the woman and made her an equal partner with the man so that she can fulfill His purposes for her and develop all the gifts that He has given her. He has freed her from the effects of sin and from the oppression that says she is inferior to men. However, now that she has been set free, she has to guard against oppressing *herself*. How? By *doing* at the expense of *being*.

The world tells us to prove our worth by what we accomplish. The Bible tells us to accept our worth in the One who loves us. You don't have to justify your worth by how much you are doing for others or how many activities you are engaged in:

> *For you did not receive a spirit that makes you a slave again to fear, but you received the Spirit of sonship. And by him we cry, "Abba, Father." The Spirit himself testifies with our spirit that we are God's children.*
>
> (Romans 8:15)

A WOMAN NEEDS TO FIND HER IDENTITY IN CHRIST. A woman first needs to find her identity in who she is in Christ—God's beloved child. It is only as she does this that she can be fulfilled and carry out His plans for her. When a woman submits to God, Christ will work in her and through her by His Spirit. In this way, she will be enabled to fulfill all the purposes He has for her—but in His strength, not her own. *"We have not received the spirit of the world but the Spirit who is from God, that we may understand what God has freely given us"* (1 Corinthians 2:12).

The woman of Proverbs 31 is not just a busy woman. She is a woman who knows her purpose in God. For example,

+ She knows that she is to trust God and draw her strength from Him so that she will not be paralyzed by anxiety; her family and others with whom she is in relationship will be able to put their confidence in her; they will know she has their best interests in mind (vv. 11–15).

+ She knows that God values her abilities and intelligence, and so she is free to pursue opportunities and make plans for expanding her realm of influence (vv. 16–18, 24).

+ She knows that God is her ultimate Source and desires to bless her, so she sets about her work with energy and anticipation. She has a good attitude and doesn't complain (v. 17).

+ Since God has blessed her, she desires to be a blessing to others, and she reaches out to those less fortunate than she (v. 20).

+ Because she knows that her worth comes from her position in God, she treats herself with respect (v. 25).

+ She has immersed herself in God's Word in order to know His ways, and therefore she is able to give godly wisdom and instruction to others. She honors Jesus with her life (v. 26).

+ Because she has come to know the God of all encouragement, she is an encouragement to her husband, children, friends, and coworkers and invests herself in their lives (verse 28).

Many women do noble things, but you surpass them all. (v. 31)

I wholeheartedly encourage you to pursue all of God's purposes for you. He created your spirit out of His being and out of His love. He designed you perfectly to fulfill your calling in Him. Accept the freedom He has given you in Christ. Know that you are esteemed by Him. Develop the creative ideas He has given you in your innermost being. Use the many gifts and talents He has placed within you. Be the blessing to yourself, your family, and your community that He created you to be.

Yet most of all, discover that not only was your spirit created out of God, but also that *"your life is now hidden with Christ in God"* (Colossians 3:2).

Your place is with and in Him.

CONCLUSION STUDY QUESTIONS

QUESTIONS FOR REFLECTION

1. On what do you base your self-worth?

2. How high a priority is the development of godly character in your life? Why?

EXPLORING GOD'S PRINCIPLES AND PURPOSES

3. Why was the woman created? (p. 229)

4. What does a woman's relationship with the Lord and the development of His character in her life do for her? (p. 229)

5. In some ways, a woman may derive her self-esteem from her _____ almost as much as a man derives his self-image from his work. (p. 229)

6. A woman wants to feel that she is _____ for the contribution she is making to her family and her community. (p. 229)

7. A woman has to guard against _____ at the expense of _____. (p. 230)

8. What two primary things does a woman need to do in order to be fulfilled and carry out God's plans for her? (p. 230)

9. Think about the qualities exhibited by the woman of Proverbs 31 in the context of what you have learned about God's plan for the woman. What examples can you give from this portion of Scripture that show this woman knows her purpose in God? (pp. 230–231)

10. Not only was the woman's spirit drawn from God, but, when she is redeemed, her life is also "_____ _____ _____ _____ _____" (Colossians 3:2). (p. 231)

11. Ultimately, a woman's place is with and in _____. (p. 231)

CONCLUSION

The world tells us to prove our worth by what we accomplish. Therefore, many women may be tempted to fill their lives with and derive their self-esteem from activities alone—even activities that serve others. Yet the Bible tells us that women are to find their worth in the One who created and redeemed them, and who loves them deeply.

God perfectly designed the woman to fulfill her calling in Him. When she accepts the freedom God has given her in Christ and knows that she is esteemed by Him, then she can live in His purposes, develop the creative ideas He has given her, and use the many gifts and talents He has placed within her. She will be a blessing to herself, her family, her community, and her world—just as He created her to be.

APPLYING GOD'S PRINCIPLES TO YOUR LIFE
THINKING IT OVER

+ Do you find that your times of prayer, Bible study, and fellowship with the Lord get squeezed out in the midst of all your many responsibilities and activities? What can you do to prevent this from happening?

+ Think about the godly character that the woman of Proverbs 31 developed and the ministry she had toward others because she knew her purpose in God. How could your life be more effective if you lived more fully in your relationship with God and the purposes He has for you?

PRAYING ABOUT IT

+ Wisdom, strength, purposefulness, and effectiveness in life come from having a vital relationship with God through Christ. Ask God to give you a hunger for Himself and His Word. Decide today to give your relationship with God first priority in your life so that you can be open to receiving His guidance and help and can better meet your responsibilities in your home, workplace, and community.

+ If you have been trying to live for God in your own strength or have been looking to your activities for validation, ask God to show you your true identity as His child and as a participant in His nature and purposes. Yield yourself to God and allow Christ to work in you and through you by His Spirit.

ACTING ON GOD'S TRUTH

+ What godly character qualities do you need to develop? List them below and then yield yourself to God, asking Him to develop these qualities within you. Review them each day, and ask God to show you how to put them into practice in your life.

+ As you near the completion of this study, perhaps you have never taken the step of restoring your relationship with your Creator. Without that relationship, you won't be able to fulfill your true purpose in life. If you haven't yet done so, come to God now, praying a prayer similar to this one:

> My Creator and God,
>
> I recognize that I need a relationship with You. I am separated from You because the first man and woman disobeyed You and rejected Your ways, and I myself have done the same. However, I also recognize that You sent Your Son, the Lord Jesus Christ, to be my Substitute and to pay for my sins and disobedience by His death on the cross. I acknowledge that You raised Him from the dead and that, because He lives, I am spiritually raised with Him to new life in You. I am now a child of God and can live in the plans and purposes for which I was created and redeemed. I will live eternally with You.

Thank you for doing all this for me because of your great love and grace. I pray this in the name of Jesus, my Savior. Amen.

Now that you are reconciled with God and have become His child, all His promises and purposes are yours through Christ. To learn how to love and serve God, read His Word and pray every day. Become involved in a local church and seek ways to serve your family and others through your God-given gifts and talents. If you are doing this study in a group setting, tell your group leader that you have prayed this prayer and ask him or her to explain more about how you can grow in your faith. God bless you as you begin the most important relationship of your life and seek to live in God's great purposes and plans for you—becoming the person He always meant for you to be.

"We have not received the spirit of the world but the Spirit who is from God, that we may understand what God has freely given us."
—1 Corinthians 2:12

ABOUT THE AUTHOR

Dr. Myles Munroe (1954–2014) was an international motivational speaker, best-selling author, educator, leadership mentor, and consultant for government and business. Traveling extensively throughout the world, Dr. Munroe addressed critical issues affecting the full range of human, social, and spiritual development. The central theme of his message is the maximization of individual potential, including the transformation of followers into leaders and leaders into agents of change.

Dr. Munroe was founder and president of Bahamas Faith Ministries International (BFMI), a multidimensional organization headquartered in Nassau, Bahamas. He was chief executive officer and chairman of the board of the International Third World Leaders Association and president of the International Leadership Training Institute.

Dr. Munroe was also the founder and executive producer of a number of radio and television programs aired worldwide. In addition, he was a frequent guest on other television and radio programs and international networks and was a contributing writer for various Bible editions, journals, magazines, and newsletters, such as *The Believer's Topical Bible*, *The African Cultural Heritage Topical Bible*, *Charisma Life Christian Magazine*, and *Ministries Today*. He was a popular author of more than forty books, including *The Power of Character in Leadership*, *The Purpose and Power of Authority*, *The Principles and Benefits of Change*, *Becoming a Leader*, *The Most Important Person on Earth*, *The Spirit of Leadership*, *The Principles and Power of Vision*, *Understanding the Purpose and Power of Prayer*, *Understanding the Purpose and Power of Women*, and *Understanding the Purpose and Power of Men*. Dr. Munroe has changed the lives of multitudes around the world with a powerful message that inspires, motivates, challenges, and empowers people to discover personal purpose, develop true potential, and manifest their unique leadership abilities. For over thirty years, he trained tens of thousands of leaders in business, industry, education, government, and religion. He personally addressed over 500,000 people each year on personal and professional development. His appeal and message transcend age, race, culture, creed, and economic background.

Dr. Munroe earned B.A. and M.A. degrees from Oral Roberts University and the University of Tulsa, and was awarded a number of honorary doctoral degrees. He also served as an adjunct professor of the Graduate School of Theology at Oral Roberts University.

The parents of two adult children, Charisa and Chairo (Myles Jr.), Dr. Munroe and his wife, Ruth, traveled as a team and were involved in teaching seminars together. Both were leaders who ministered with sensitive hearts and international vision. In November 2014, they were tragically killed in an airplane crash en route to an annual leadership conference sponsored by Bahamas Faith Ministries International. A statement from Dr. Munroe in his book *The Power of Character in Leadership* summarizes his own legacy: "Remember that character ensures the longevity of leadership, and men and women of principle will leave important legacies and be remembered by future generations."

Welcome to Our House!

We Have a Special Gift for You

It is our privilege and pleasure to share in your love of Christian books. We are committed to bringing you authors and books that feed, challenge, and enrich your faith.

To show our appreciation, we invite you to sign up to receive a specially selected **Reader Appreciation Gift**, with our compliments. Just go to the Web address at the bottom of this page.

God bless you as you seek a deeper walk with Him!

WHITAKER
HOUSE